By Rich Cohen

THE LAST PIRATE OF NEW YORK

THE LAST
PIRATE
of New York

A Ghost Ship, a Killer, and the Birth of a Gangster Nation

RICH COHEN

SPI
EGE
L & G
RAU

SPIEGEL & GRAU

New York

Published in the United States by Spiegel & Grau, an imprint of Random House, a division of Penguin Random House LLC, New York.

SPIEGEL & GRAU and colophon is a registered trademark of Penguin Random House LLC.

LIBRARY OF CONGRESS CATALOGING-IN-PUBLICATION DATA
Names: Cohen, Rich, author.
Title: The last pirate of New York : a ghost ship, a killer, and the birth of a gangster nation / by Rich Cohen.
Description: First edition. | New York : Spiegel & Grau, 2019. |
Includes bibliographical references and index.
Identifiers: LCCN 2018049488 | ISBN 9780399589928 (hbk : alk. paper) |
ISBN 9780399589935 (ebook)
Subjects: LCSH: Hicks, Albert W., approximately 1820–1860. | Criminals—New York (State)—Biography. | Pirates—New York (State)—Biography.
Classification: LCC HV6248.H4527 C64 2019 | DDC 364.1092 [B]—dc23
LC record available at https://lccn.loc.gov/2018049488

Printed in the United States of America on acid-free paper

randomhousebooks.com
spiegelandgrau.com

2 4 6 8 9 7 5 3 1

First Edition

Book design by Debbie Glasserman

To Jessica,
even when the valve narrows
and the walls cave in

Well, it may be the devil or it may be the Lord
But you're gonna have to serve somebody.

—BOB DYLAN

CONTENTS

THE LAST PIRATE OF NEW YORK

ONCE UPON A TIME

I grew up on gangster stories. While other kids were hearing about the Three Little Pigs and the Old Woman Who Lived in a Shoe, my father was telling me about the legends of his New York childhood—Pittsburgh Phil Strauss and Louis "Lepke" Buchalter, Lucky Luciano and Meyer Lansky, the visionary who put craps up on a table. "The lesson here," my father said softly, as I lay in bed, "is that it was the same game, just played on a different level."

For a kid in the suburbs, these stories were more than stories. They were redbrick stoops, air shafts crossed by clotheslines, alleys, candy stores and subterranean club rooms, apartment houses that, compared to my atomized world of detached single-family living, seemed like paradise—coastal Brooklyn, where the fog bathes everything in a ghostly light and the Verrazzano-Narrows Bridge vanishes halfway across, like a ladder with its top in the clouds.

As soon as I was old enough, I moved to New York. I said I was looking for a job, but I had really come in search of the truth behind my father's stories. This became my career. Parents: be careful what you tell your children at night. I explored the parts of the city where I knew the old-time gangsters had operated: Little Italy and the Lower East Side, East New York and Brownsville, Brooklyn, the piers that had been the heart of the old Fourth Ward. I was consumed by New York history—not the story of marble buildings and glad-handing mayors but the alternate story that ran parallel and beneath—the story of the underworld, its heroes and stool pigeons, founders and visionaries. As my father said, "the same game, just played on a different level."

In time, mostly but not entirely working in my capacity as a reporter, I came to know some living examples of the genus and species: New York gangster. The young toughs loitering in front of the Ravenite Social Club on Mulberry Street circa 1990. Outer-borough boys done up like canaries, in yellow and green. And, still more interesting, the old-timers who'd started their careers when the last of the ancients were still throwing lightning bolts. I spent an afternoon shadowing one of the men around St. Vincent's Triangle in the Village asking about the way things used to be. They said he was feeble-minded, but that was an act. I found another gangster in New Jersey. ("I can't handle you in town," he said. "Meet me at the Meadowlands Complex. That's mine. From there to Asbury Park, it all belongs to me.") He said he'd talk to me, "'cause I met your father at La Costa, and he treat me real cordial." When I told my father, he said, "If you write about Johnny, write nice. If he doesn't like it, it's not a letter to the editor he's gonna send." I met a boss of bosses, *capo di tutti capi,* at Bert Young's restaurant on East Gun Hill Road in the Bronx. Dozens of members of the Genovese crime family had been arrested and made bail and were celebrating. The boss knew my book *Tough Jews,* the first installment of this grander gangster project. The story of the Brooklyn mob Murder Inc., it centered on Abe "Kid Twist" Reles, who, after testifying against members of his own gang, was tossed out a window of the Half Moon Hotel on Coney Island. He was dubbed "The Canary Who Could Sing But Couldn't Fly."

"I wouldn't put him in my fuckin' book," the boss told me. "Maybe it's history, but Reles was nothing but a goddamn rat."

When I asked the boss who he would put in his book, he smiled and said, "There are so many."

I suddenly realized that these men had also grown up on gangster stories told by their fathers. The boss recalled some of them, then encouraged me to track down the biographies. When I did, I found still other men who'd been raised on gangster stories. No matter how far back I went, in fact, I found still older old-timers talking about still more ancient days. It was an infinite regress. It went on and on, fading to an age so distant, it was lit by kerosene lamp. It gave me a mission, inspired a quest: I would track down and name and chronicle the very first New York gangster, the man behind all the other legends.

Many consider Monk Eastman to have been the first. He led a gang called the Eastmans, had a pocked face and scary eyes, fought battles on Orchard and Cherry streets, served in the First World War, and was found dead outside a dance hall on Fourteenth Street in 1920. But when Eastman turned up in the dives, old-timers were already telling stories about gangsters of an earlier generation. If you figured out who those gangsters were actually talking about, you'd establish the bedrock beneath the underworld, the source of all that criminal energy. You might come to understand the alchemical process that turns psychopaths into folk heroes. You might even unlock something fundamental about New York. In this way, lantern in hand, I continued until I reached the Mesozoic era of the Manhattan underworld, when the earliest mobsters emerged from the primordial ooze. Little Augie Fein, gunned down on the corner of Norfolk and Delancey; Mose, the otherwise nameless thug who would pass his cigar to an underling before a fight, saying, "Hold de butt"; Bill "the Butcher" Poole, whose last words were, "Good-bye, boys, I die a true American!" These were some of the first bad men—but who were they telling stories about at bedtime?

Albert Hicks is the closest thing the New York underworld has to a Cain, the first killer and the first banished man, carrying that dread mark: MURDER. He operated so long ago, in a city so similar to and yet so different from our own, the word *gangster* had not yet been coined. He was called a pirate.

For years, he operated out of the public eye, rambling from crime to crime, working under an alias, sleeping in the nickel-a-night flops that filled the lower part of Manhattan, drinking in barrooms where the great entertainments were rat-baiting and bear-baiting—patrons wagered on how many rats a terrier could kill, on how many dogs it would take to bring down a bear. In 1860

Hicks was New York's most feared man. This was Manhattan as dark fairy tale, an early draft that would be overwritten until it became a palimpsest. Even now, everywhere you look, reminders of that ancient city bleed through: at Peck Slip and the East River, a neighborhood once lousy with tall ships, blind pigs, and sons of bitches, a pirates' playground; at Hangman's Elm in Washington Square Park, a three-hundred-year-old tree said to have once served as a gallows for public executions; at Stillwell Avenue and the Boardwalk in Coney Island, where Lucky Luciano sat his boss Joe Masseria at a poker table, then stepped aside as a squad of hitmen, including Bugsy Siegel and Joe Adonis, came through the door. Asked where he'd been during the shooting, Luciano told police, "Taking a pee; I always took a long pee."

Hicks came to New York to make his fortune. He did it in crime, but he can stand as an alter ego for all those strivers who reach the city in search of success. He worked on the water; he worked in ships. He became notorious in the worst neighborhood Manhattan had ever known, the Five Points, where Anthony Street, Orange Street, and Cross Street came together to form the edge of Paradise Square. That New York was a sugar-and-salt mix of politics, business, and brutality. We know about the early political leaders: Peter Stuyvesant and Fernando Wood. We know about the pioneering tycoons: Cornelius Vanderbilt and J. P. Morgan. Albert Hicks was a founding father same as them, only he was a founder of New York's underworld. His story was passed down by word of mouth, told and retold until it became a legend. It was officially recorded just once—in the press, as it unfolded—then shifted from breaking news to tall tale, added to and tarted up as time passed. If it's not been properly chronicled since the summer of 1860, it's partly because these events took place on the eve of the Civil War. That conflagration overhangs this story like the shadow of an incoming comet. In a moment, everything would be blown away.

To research these events, I relied on police records, court documents, and newspaper accounts. The spirit of the time is less in the details of those articles than in the tone, the cacophony of voices, the competitive jostling between the *New York Herald,* the *New York Sun,* the *Brooklyn Daily Eagle,* and the *New York Times.* There were dozens of daily papers, evening and morning editions, as well as weeklies that offered deeper analysis. In obsessing on Hicks, in reading the old books and newspaper columns, I came to understand the city in a new way. All the good and all the bad were already in place in 1860. Everything that's happened since has merely been a dreamlike elaboration.

Even contemporaneous writers knew Albert Hicks was something other than a normal killer. He was a demon. He had that kind of charisma. He put his arm around the town and pulled its people close. In writing about him, reporters of the time were capturing a new kind of terror—the terror of the metropolis, its anonymity, all those tenements and all those windows, all those docks and all those harborside taverns, all those numbered streets and all those mysterious lives. Albert Hicks personified the free-wheeling city that would have to make way for the modern metropolis. He was Manhattan as it had been when pirates anchored off Fourteenth Street. The hero of the lunatics, a first citizen of a criminal nation, the subject of ancient bloody bedtime tales.

His final spree played out like a ghost story, only it happened to be true.

U.S. Ship *Portsmouth*

THE GHOST SHIP

The ship was spotted March 21, 1860—Wednesday, four hours before dawn—by the crew of the *J. R. Mather*, a schooner hauling molasses to Philadelphia. The captain of the *Mather*, Ben Nickerson, discovered the ship by running into it. *Bang!* The crew was sent reeling. Nickerson rushed to the bridge. That's when he saw the strange sloop, a dark shape on dark water, listing as if wounded. The bowsprit—the spar that extends from the prow over the sea—had snapped off. The fore-topmast staysail, inner jib, outer jib, and flying jib had come down in a heap. Wood and rigging landed on the deck of the *Mather*, where Nickerson stood over it, muttering. He went to work untangling the mess. His first reaction was anger. Why had this ghost been drifting without lights in the center of the Lower Bay? But when he turned his attention to the sloop, anger gave way to dread. There was something unreal about the ship. No sound came from it, no sign of life. No glow came from the pilothouse, no sailors stood at the rail. The decks were deserted.

Nickerson called out—shouted, helloed—but nothing came back. Speaking to police a few days later, he recalled the unsettling silence. He would have investigated further had his own boat not been badly damaged. He returned for repairs to the South Street docks on the East River in Lower Manhattan instead, bringing with him the first news of the mysterious ship. That report, as well as the rigging Nickerson had carried away from the collision, fired up the rumor mill. Within hours, the story was being told in every harborside tavern.

New York was a maritime city. It was all about the waterfront, oyster sloops and ferries, steamships and cutters, channels, tidal washes, and bays. Nearly everyone below Houston Street was connected to the ocean. Terms like *bowsprit* did not have to be defined; nor did *forecastle, rigging,* or *captain's daughter.* Everyone knew the bowsprit was the spar that extended over the sea, that the forecastle was the ship's upper deck before the mast, that the rigging was the system of ropes that controlled the sails, that a captain's daughter was the whip that officers used to discipline unruly sailors, as in, "All right, boys, give him the captain's daughter." In that New York, an abandoned sloop, without crew or direction, a phantom nearly within sight of the downtown docks yet lost in a watery delirium, stood for breakdown and chaos.

The crew of the *Telegraph*, a schooner out of New London, Connecticut, were the first to get a good look at the ghost ship. The sailors spotted it less than an hour after the collision with the *J. R. Mather*. The ghost was already a kind of ruin. Bowsprit busted, sails down, adrift—a thing like that is a bad omen, a portent of evil. They saw it at first light. The captain of the *Telegraph* recorded the location: the Lower Bay, between Brooklyn's West Bank and Romer Shoals, an outcrop that stands between the harbor and the open sea.

The *Telegraph* sailed around the ghost ship, the crew calling out, looking for signs of life, then tied to it. Several men went on board to investigate. The ghost was identified by the name on its side: *E. A. Johnson*. It was a classic oyster sloop, a mast in the middle, a main sail and smaller sails in front and in back. The crew of the *Telegraph* walked the deck, then went down the ladder to the cabin, bewildered by everything they saw. Ax marks in the ceiling and floor, drawers pulled out, locks smashed, trails of blood and pools of blood that ran in rivulets when the ship pitched. An oyster sloop was typically crewed by four to six, yet no bodies could be found. "Her deck appeared to have been washed in human blood," the captain of the *Telegraph* said later.

The yawl, the wood rowboat that served as life raft and dinghy on every sloop, was missing. Here were the braces and here were the chains, but the boat itself was gone.

The *Telegraph* tried to tow the *E. A. Johnson* back to the city, but it was too heavy, and the sea was too rough. The captain called for help. Dozens of tugboats worked in the harbor, clearing wrecks, shepherding traffic. The *Ceres,* commanded by Captain Stevens, sat as low as the tugboat in the children's story, red and gold, funnel and smokestack, pilothouse topped by a huge American flag—thirty-three stars. Captain Stevens boarded the ghost, walked the decks, and saw the signs of the slaughter, then shook off whatever unease he might be feeling and got to work. After securing the sloop with ropes and chains, he pushed it through the Narrows and Upper Bay, which was among the deepest, most protected natural harbors in the world. The *E. A. Johnson* drew attention from every onlooker—a battered craft, broken and bleeding, touched by disaster.

Trinity Church was the tallest building in Manhattan. Its spire could be seen before anything else, rising out of the sea. Then the harbor islands, the clanging buoys, and the seagull-covered rocks. Then Manhattan, with its warehouses and exchanges, wooden tenements and narrow streets.

The *Ceres* left the *E. A. Johnson* at a pier beside the Fulton Fish Market, where the morning rush had given way to a sleepy afternoon. The warehouses were built on piers over the East River, brackish, trash-filled water sloshing around the posts. The market had opened in 1822 and would stay in that location—between Fulton and Beekman streets on the East River—until 2005, making it, for many years, the longest continuously operating shopping center in the United States. Sloops and draggers unloaded their catch through the night, and trading began at dawn. The stalls were heaped high with shellfish and finfish, many still alive, gasping through bloodied gills. The sky above the market was awash in seagulls, screaming and turning great circles.

Crowds soon assembled to look at the ghost ship: cold-faced men in hats, street urchins, sailors, and clerks.

They'd heard the rumors via the lightning-fast word-of-mouth network that carries news around all seaports.

The story made the late editions of the newspapers. By the next morning, it was the topic of every conversation.

The police went to work as soon as the sloop was anchored. Captain Hart Weed and an officer named Washbourne walked over to the Fulton Fish Market from the second precinct station house at 49 Beekman. They examined the wreckage on the *Telegraph,* ropes and rigging—it was docked nearby—then went aboard the *E. A. Johnson.* Then came the coroner—Schirmer—who wrote everything down in a book. The cops started at the prow of the *E. A. Johnson* in full sight of the crowd. "The deck was besmeared with blood," Captain Weed said later. "It appeared as if two persons had been lying on it, and one had been dragged out of the cabin; the appearance of the blood led to the inference that on deck one had lain in front of the mast, and the other amidships. . . . Forward of the mast there was some light-colored hair and blood; the blood had run on both sides of the vessel; when [we] hauled the sail up it was found to have covered up a great quantity of blood. . . . On two places there were blood outside the rail, rubbed on, as if a bleeding body with clothes on had been thrown overboard."

The cabin was in disarray—everything smashed. The floor, according to Captain Weed, looked as if it had been "scrubbed with water; there was a pail there which looked as if there had been bloody water in it, and the rope by which the pail was dipped into the water was saturated with blood, and had hair on it; the blood and hair were near the end of the rope, which was about six feet long— long enough to dip into the water from over the vessel's side; there was no water in the pail, but the rope was wet; I found a broom, and it had the appearance of having been used to brush the blood into the forepart of the cabin, behind the stove."

Captain Weed discovered three holes "bored" into the floor behind the stove. These holes had been made with a hot poker—Weed called it an "augur"—found nearby. The purpose, some believed, was to fill the cabin with water and sink the ship. It seemed evidence of intent—a man meant to hide his crimes by sending the sloop to the bottom of the harbor. But blood had rushed out instead, carrying detritus that stopped up the holes and saved the *E. A. Johnson.*

Captain Weed found a shirt on a dressing table. He held it up, letting it fall open. It was covered in slashes— four or five at least—each showing a place a blade went in. He reported:

> The biggest [slash] was seven inches. I found also that the walls and ceiling were besmeared with blood, and the gashes in the ceiling above appeared to have been done with a knife. I should suppose that the ceiling of the cabin is about six or eight inches higher than I am (that is, it is about 6 feet 4 inches at the most;) there was blood on the side of the cabin door, which (the blood) had the appearance of being fresh and seemed to have spurted on each side as the person bleeding was being hauled

out; there was a new sail on top of the stairs, on removing which we found two lockers that had the appearance of being searched; we found a hole under the stairs, in which was contained the lead-line and some other articles; the blood had run down there, quite a quantity of it; when the sail was pulled out you could, by getting on your knees and crawling under, get at the private locker; on searching the drawer there, we found some blank papers, and papers not of that crew but of the crews of former voyages.

By following the blood, the police got a picture of bodies falling, lying, being dragged. The search ended at the rail on the starboard side, where Weed found a bloody handprint. It looked as if a man had clung to the wood, as if hanging on for life.

Weed noticed something else. "Look," he said.

The men got on their haunches. There, on deck, was all that remained of the crew of the *E. A. Johnson*—four severed fingers and a thumb.

Manhattan island lies within an estuary. It's where the currents converge, where a tidal wash (the East River) meets a cataract (the Hudson River, formerly called the North River), a flood of sweet water that runs down from the mountains. New York Harbor is a network of islands and coves, seabirds and arsenical green marshland, the sort that looks solid until you step on it. The Hudson, turbid and overshadowed by palisades, deepens below Manhattan. In the old days, every road on the island ended at the water, the sun rose at the foot of every street. Even now, when the fog rolls in, the waterfront is a sailor's dream.

The town grew around the harbor. In the late 1600s, all housing and commerce were crowded in tight communion on the southern shore. It was a fishing village and a trading post, then a bustling military base, a fort on the edge of an unknown continent, then a small town, then a big town, then a small city, then a metropolis. In 1860 New York was among the richest ports in the world. Hundreds of millions of dollars of produce and machinery sat in its warehouses. Its coast was girdled by wharves; more than a hundred piers studded the East River and North River. The population doubled, then doubled again. Huge ships carried immigrant Irish and Germans into the city, a harbinger of the Jews and Poles and Russians and Italians who would follow. The inspection station at Ellis Island was not opened until 1892. In 1860, when this story takes place, emigrants were still landing in Manhattan and being processed through Castle Garden, an antique brownstone fort beside the Battery, where the Dutch had kept their big guns. As respectable neighborhoods turned into vast immigrant slums, Manhattan approached a mystical number—one million inhabitants.

Such a city is about traffic control: regular ferry service had quickly been established with every important river and seaport in the Northeast. In addition, there was a twice-weekly run to Liverpool, England, huge steamships carrying the wealth of the American South, cargoes of cotton that powered Britain's industrial economy. A black market in slaves flourished in the shadow of the harbor: pirates, violating the ban on the international

slave trade, smuggled human beings from the west coast of Africa to New York, where they were sold, transferred, and carried to Baltimore, Charleston, Savannah, and New Orleans. There was a booming trade in guns and narcotics. Mott and Pell streets would soon be riddled with opium dens, subbasement cellars with velvet couches where hopheads took the curling white smoke deep into their lungs, their stony eyes filling with clouds and clipper ships. Whatever you wanted could be had in the riverfront taverns. On Water Street, you walked beneath the bowsprits of dozens of foreign ships, an artificial forest so thick it made a kind of canopy.

Merchants, bartenders, and stage performers, bankers, cops, and criminals—especially criminals: everyone lived off the sailors who pumped through the city like blood. Most of these criminals, and most of their crimes, were confined to a handful of neighborhoods, the famous slums of New York. The Five Points, ur-ghetto of urban

America, a sprawl of old barns and factories, tenements leaning this way and that. Charles Dickens had written about it:

> Here, too are lanes and alleys, paved with mud knee-deep: underground chambers, where they dance and game; the walls bedecked with rough designs of ships, and forts, and flags, and American eagles out of number: ruined houses, open to the street, whence, through wide gaps in the walls, other ruins loom upon the eye, as though the world of vice and misery had nothing else to show: hideous tenements which take their name from robbery and murder; all that is loathsome, drooping, and decayed is here.

As had Davy Crockett:

> It appeared as if the cellars were jam full of people; and such fiddling and dancing nobody ever before saw in this world. . . . Black and white, white and black, hugemsnug together, happy as lords and ladies, sitting sometimes round in a ring, with a jug of liquor between them, and I do think I saw more drunken folks, men and women, that day than I ever saw before. . . . I thought I would rather risk myself in an Indian fight than venture among these creatures after night.

Most New Yorkers led sensible, hardworking lives. They rented houses and apartments in the center of the island, as far as possible from the raucous waterfront.

The rich lived still farther uptown, in mansions on suburban Fifth Avenue. Central Park opened to the public in 1858. But the real action, the color and excitement, the fashion, music, and night life, was in the slums, the greatest being the Five Points. It was built on the grave of an ancient pond, the Collect, once New York City's main source of drinking water. Befouled by industry, the Collect was drained in the early 1800s, then covered with streets and buildings, but the fill had not been done properly, and the buildings sagged and the basements filled with water. Understandably, the inhabitants of such a neighborhood, beaten and abandoned, championed anyone who seemed to defy the city's aristocratic powers.

The Five Points bred many of the town's first street gangs, ethnic armies that went to war with each other and with the world. These were less like modern mob outfits—less like the famous Five Families—than like medieval peasant bands. They had little organization, method, or plan. The order of the day was simple: maraud. The names of these gangs are a hymn of colorful decay: the Whyos, the Chichesters, the Forty Thieves, the Plug Uglies, the Dead Rabbits, the Hudson Dusters. The toughest worked in the Sixth Ward, which covered a few dozen acres between Broadway and the Bowery. The grid of numbered streets and lettered avenues was laid out in the early 1800s, but it was still the old New York down here, with bends and hooks and rookeries and lanes. Many streets followed the path of a lost Indian trail or the shore of a vanished lake. Everything was evidence of something that was gone. Cherry Street had once been among the city's grandest thoroughfares. It's where George Washington was inaugurated, where John Han-

cock and DeWitt Clinton lived. It was dotted with parks
and stately homes, but cut-rate developers filled the lots
with tenements. By 1860, the old mansions had decayed.
Many had been turned into bordellos or flophouses. In
thirty years, the Sixth Ward had gone from leafy elegance
to urban nightmare.

The waterfront neighborhoods were even worse. Cor-
lears Hook, a jutting coast that served as a landmark for
river navigators (it's now mostly buried beneath the FDR
Drive), had been a red-light district since the early nineteenth century. By 1855 it was the heart of the local crime
scene, crowded with dance halls and saloons, including
the infamous Tub of Blood bar, home of the Tub of Blood
Bunch and the even more infamous Hole-in-the-Wall Saloon, the headquarters of a gang called the Hookers.

The characteristic crime of New York City's
nineteenth-century waterfront was the shanghai. Because
conditions aboard sailing vessels were both boring and
brutal, some part of every crew fled as soon as a ship
reached port, leaving whalers and sloops short of man-
power. Post a notice, interview seamen—that was the
proper way. But desperate captains often hired port
agents, disreputable characters, to kidnap drunks from
waterfront crimps. At these run-down hotels, an agent
would comb the lobby bar for a mark. At some point, he
would dose the mark's drink with a mickey—usually lau-
danum, which was one part opium and many parts Canary wine. When the mark stumbled to bed to sleep it off,
the agent followed with a blackjack, then delivered the
blow that sent the mark into deep unconsciousness. The
most storied crimps, such as the Old Fourth Ward Hotel
at Catherine and Water streets, were built on piers with

trapdoors that led directly from the bedrooms to the river, where a rowboat was waiting. By the time the mark awoke hours or even days later, he was on a ship at sea. The choice was simple: work or swim. In the worst case, such a man would end up on a whaler bound for China— "shanghaied"—which meant he would be away for four or five months, like dropping off the map; his wife might grieve for a time, then marry another. Hundreds of marks were kidnapped in the Fourth Ward in the 1850s and '60s.

All kinds of criminals operated along the East River. Child crooks, apprentice pickpockets, served as lures. Most established gangs had a youth auxiliary for this purpose. The Forty Thieves had the Forty Little Thieves. The Hudson Dusters had the Little Hudson Dusters. Members of child gangs had tough faces, wore ragged coats and patched pants, and were underfed, illiterate, disease-ridden, and mean. They lived three to a bed in tenement flops, stalked the streets, and drank turpentine on a dare. There were con artists, bunko men, crooked dealers in every kind of card game—faro, poker, stud. There were thousands of gang members: some joined because they wanted a family, some because they needed protection. There were pimps and hookers, loan sharks, opium dealers, and addicts.

And pirates. An 1850 police report estimated the presence of between four hundred and five hundred pirates in New York City. To the police, a pirate was any criminal who made his living on the water, attacking and robbing ships beyond the jurisdiction of the landlocked coppers—named for the tin badge on their peaked caps. Most river pirates were boys, twelve to eighteen years old, divided among a dozen or so outfits. The Slaughter Housers worked out of Slaughter House Point; the Patsy Conroys worshipped their martyred founder; the Short Tails were known for their favorite kind of coat; the Swamp Angels, the Hookers, the Border Gang, the Buckoos, and the Daybreak Boys—so called because that's when they emerged in their flat-bottom boats—hit the sloops in the harbor, then vanished into the sewers.

Then there was that more mysterious category of criminal, a man—always a man—who lived between these worlds, engaged in a mission of his own. Freelancers and solo operators, these thugs were so feared, they did not require the protection of any gang. People left them alone because who needed that kind of trouble?

Two weeks before the *E. A. Johnson* was found ghosting, Albert Hicks was sitting alone in a Water Street saloon—the Hole-in-the-Wall, say, with its card tables and its long oaken bar. For a nickel, drinking through a tube from a cask, you could take in all the beer you could hold. A man hammered out popular tunes on a rickety piano. The front door was a few hundred yards from the docks. You could hear foghorns, and maybe a sailor singing in a crow's nest.

Hicks was big and broad-shouldered—"strongly built" was how the police put it—a shade under six feet tall, with high cheekbones and wide-set black eyes that were described, variously, as accusatory, suspicious, paranoid, and wild. He'd let his beard grow, but it was mostly stubble beneath the chin. He was dark, tanned by many years at sea. Those who met him later, or who took him in from the safe side of the jailhouse bars, came away surprised—a man who lived as he did, who did what he'd done, should not have been handsome. It didn't seem right. At some point, after a second or third whiskey, his expression would go from amused to dangerous. If you met his gaze, you'd regret it.

No one knew much about him. The reporters said only that he'd been married and had a child and had spent years working on ships. He lived nearby and often drank alone. They said he could neither read nor write—his wife read to him from the newspaper—but not everyone believed it. He seemed to understand even the small print when it was in his interest.

He'd spent his early years on a farm in Foster, Rhode Island, one of eleven siblings. Simon, the firstborn, became notorious before Albert. He'd befriended an old man in Foster, spent hours in his company. Then late one night he sneaked into the old man's house, killed him in his bed, stole his money, went to Providence, and had a spree. Captured, tried, convicted, and sentenced to hang, he escaped in a jailbreak and was never seen again. Where did Simon Hicks go? Out west, probably, where there was no law. It was a story that stayed with Albert, a story with a lesson moral. Even in the last moment, when you have nothing ahead but a swinging rope, you still have the possibility of escape.

Hicks was a Freemason—that's one of the few facts that suggest his internal life and beliefs. He joined the secret brotherhood somewhere along the way, perhaps attracted by the comity of a lodge or by the ritual and mystical explanation. To a Freemason, the world is an allegory shot through with symbols and signs meant to lead the faithful toward enlightenment. These hints are complicated and interlocked, like wheels within wheels, set in place by a hidden power. To Hicks, it would have suggested the existence of at least two worlds: one where things were as they appeared, and another where all the usual meanings were inverted. In that second world, the criminal was the hero and the condemned man was king.

In the 1850s Hicks was a terrifying presence in lower Manhattan, a fiend of the taverns and dives. Some accounts described him as the most feared criminal on the waterfront—"the baddest man." Sitting at the bar, he would stare into space or into his glass—wine so red it was black—laughing quietly. Stories followed him. Some said he'd fought with the gangs in the old days, when it was all tribal warfare below Fourteenth Street. Some said he'd hired himself out to various bosses, working for whoever was willing to pay most, fighting first for the Daybreak Boys, then for the Chichesters. Some said he'd operated as a hit man—you paid him, your problem went away. Asked for details, a bartender at the Hole-in-the-Wall told a reporter, "I know only that he looked for ships and that he followed the sea."

It can be hard to get a clean read on Albert Hicks. Was he a prototype for the modern hit man, for Sammy "the Bull" Gravano, the mob enforcer, a menace who, once unleashed, cannot be recalled? Or was he something else, something older—the last of the pirates, the last of the Blackbeards and Jean Lafittes, a character out of Robert Louis Stevenson? He seems a kind of missing link. With him, the pirate turned into the gangster: he emerged onto dry land and took up in bars and casinos—Blackbeard morphing into Al Capone. Hicks became infamous during New York gangland's prehistory. Writing about him, reporters created a basic underworld type. He was the first swamp angel, the great-grandfather of every mob punk and Bowery psycho who would follow.

According to Herbert Asbury, author of the classic *Gangs of New York,* Hicks had been a victim before he'd become a killer, the subject of a shanghai who'd gone to sleep in a Cherry Street crimp but awakened on the *E. A. Johnson* at sea. It's not clear where Asbury got this story. Maybe he invented it, along with the quote, attributed to Hicks, that seemed to confirm it: "After I realized what had been done to me, how I'd been mistreated and taken from my wife and child, I was filled with rage. Standing at the wheel of the ship, I determined to avenge myself by murdering all hands aboard." Or maybe the shanghai story had already been part of the legend when Asbury came along—his book was published in 1928, nearly seventy years after the fact—added by raconteurs or mythmakers looking for a moral. Those who claimed Hicks had been kidnapped were seeking sympathy for the pirate, for without that sympathy he could not be fashioned into an archetype, a personification of grit. If he'd been shanghaied, his crimes would have been understandable, if not justifiable. But Hicks was not shanghaied; nor did he ever fall victim. His truth was less complicated and more terrifying. Cold, calculating, remorseless, Albert Hicks was always the hunter, never the hunted.

In the spring of 1860, he was hunting, looking for a score big enough to set up his family. He spent weeks studying manifests and want ads, walking the North and East River docks. He was searching for a certain kind of ship with a certain kind of crew engaged in a certain kind of trade. "I kept a sharp lookout for small craft outward bound for cargoes of fruit, oysters, etc., and in a quiet way gathered all the information I could in regard to the number of hands they shipped, and the amount of money they generally carried," he later explained.

He settled on the *E. A. Johnson* because it looked like a fat target. A midsize oyster sloop, it would leave New York empty, sail down the Atlantic coast to Deep Creek, Virginia, purchase a few thousand oysters, then return to the Fulton Fish Market to sell the cargo to wholesalers, who'd sell it to restaurants and fishmongers. The entire run would take two or three weeks. The cargo was fragile—oysters go bad—so the purchase would have to be made in cash. It was this cash—oyster sloops were famous for carrying it—that got the pirate's attention. Get into the lockbox on the first leg, before the money was paid out—that was the idea.

By asking around, Hicks learned the makeup of the *E. A. Johnson*'s crew—just three when Hicks inquired. Captain Burr, not yet forty years old, was a bearded fireplug in sea boots and sea coat, a pipe in the corner of his mouth, his face as dour as a face in a portrait behind a waterfront tavern. At just 135 pounds, Burr was surprisingly strong—all that loading and unloading, hauling and tying knots in the sun. He was a cord of muscle, as taut as rope. The deckhands were two half-brothers. Oliver Watts, at twenty-three, was big and strong and probably the only serious obstacle to Hicks—deal with him first. Oliver's little brother, nineteen-year-old Smith Watts, was willowy and tall, a sea-obsessed boy who'd long dreamed of following Oliver into the world. "The sloop *E. A.*

Johnson offered an easy prey," Hicks later said. "She had on board, I supposed, from all the information I could gather, something over a thousand dollars."

Captain Burr was in need of a new first mate—his top officer had quit when the sloop last arrived in New York. Hicks applied under the name William Johnson, an alias he used on many voyages. It allowed him to live a double life. Albert Hicks was a law-abiding husband with a young child. William Johnson was a remorseless pirate, the author of scores of bloody deeds.

In advance of his interview on the *E. A. Johnson,* Hicks shaved. His cheekbones were sharp, and his eyes glittered beneath his Kossuth hat—a fashion of the moment, named for the Hungarian freedom fighter who'd worn one at fiery rallies in Manhattan. Floppy-brimmed, it shaded his eyes, protecting his face. Hicks came to be identified by this hat as much as by his physical appearance. His sea coat, sometimes called a monkey coat, fell below his knees. Now and then, caught in the wind, it snapped behind him like a flag.

He answered Captain Burr's questions thoroughly but briefly. He'd always made a good impression. He had knowledge of ropes and sails—ropes would play an important role in his life—was a decent helmsman, and was willing to do repairs. He could work with wood and considered himself a skilled carpenter. He'd come with his own set of tools.

Burr hired him on the spot, then introduced him to the others. Smith and Oliver Watts were from Islip, Long Island, an Atlantic fishing village. They had the same father but different mothers. Smith had grown up the doted-on only child of that mother and nearly had to run away to get clear of the house. He was an adolescent with a wispy blond beard.

Captain Burr lived in Islip, too, though he was hardly ever at home. He kept in touch with his wife by mail. They were close in the way of people who share everything on paper. A sailor writing to his landlocked spouse— there is nothing more melancholy. Burr was half owner of the *E. A. Johnson*. He'd spent years in the service of other men, working and saving until he could buy a stake in his own vessel. It was state of the art for the time, a three-masted schooner with a large hold and a comfortable cabin, so well made you could lash a cord to the wheel and let it sail itself.

The *E. A. Johnson* could haul any sort of cargo, even be used as a dragger, but it was built for oysters; the holds were large enough for several hundred pounds of ice and fish. New York had once had the greatest oyster beds in the world, but most had been exhausted or polluted by 1840. A booming business had opened in oyster hauling—an all-cash business because of the fragility of the crop. An enterprising captain could make a dozen runs a year, sailing a circuit between Manhattan and the Carolinas, returning with several thousand pounds of James River, Nansemond River, or York Point oysters that, once transferred from the sloop to the Fulton Street market bins, would doze atop ice amid yellowtail, crab, and grouper on Fulton Street. A captain who was lucky as well as clever, could expect an income in the neighborhood of twenty thousand dollars a year.

Hicks moved onto the *Johnson* to prepare for the upcoming voyage. Several people—they'd later be called as witnesses—saw him on or near the sloop. Selah Howell, the ship's co-owner, had dinner with Captain Burr and first mate Albert Hicks while the *Johnson* was anchored at the Spring Street pier, which long ago vanished beneath industry, roads, and landfill. Howell would remember Hicks as a commanding presence, polite but taciturn. Daniel Simmons, the investor who'd funded the run, saw Hicks on deck when he, Simmons, came along with the money. "I gave the captain two hundred dollars in silver coins," Simmons said. "I paid him the balance of his charter money in gold, two tens, two fives and a two and a half, one dollar in gold and a half dollar." Simmons carried the money in a canvas sack variously described as a shot bag or a seabag. Hicks watched Captain Burr lock it below. Hicks had a full beard when Simmons saw him— dark riddled with red, as if woven in blood.

James Bacon—wharf grunt, odd-job man—had come aboard to shovel out the cargo hold, the shells and muck left over from the previous voyage. He saw Hicks at a distance but remembered his clothes: "A check shirt, a short coat, and a comforter about his neck. I think in the morning he had on a monkey coat, and when he went to work he pulled on a blue shirt."

In the days before the voyage, the sloop made several short trips. At some point, it was anchored in Gravesend Bay, on the Narrows, where Staten Island comes closest to Brooklyn. Charles Baker, who worked in Gravesend Bay, saw Hicks in "a kind of monkey coat. He had whiskers," but "none on his upper lip that I could see."

Reuben Keymer, who lived a few hundred feet from Gravesend Bay and spent evenings watching the harbor traffic, had seen Hicks in a yawl, rowing beside Smith

Watts. Keymer made eye contact with Hicks, then turned away. "I was afraid he would run afoul of me," Keymer would say in court.

Keymer happened to catch Hicks in an unguarded moment, mask down, but Captain Burr picked up none of the signals. Hicks had gone out of his way to charm the captain. "This man, William Johnson, who lives in New York, is a smart fellow," Burr wrote his wife. "He went at the mast and scraped it while we were in Keyport, without telling, while I was ashore. He is a good hand; can turn his hand to almost anything."

"We sailed on the sixteenth of March from the foot of Spring Street, and proceeded to Keyport, [Long Island]," Hicks would tell detectives. "That's where I scraped the mast of the sloop, did a lot of carpenter work, and evidently pleased Captain Burr very much." From there, the *E. A. Johnson* went to Islip, then back to Spring Street, then to Gravesend Bay (near modern Bensonhurst, with its soccer fields and its redbrick apartments) to wait for the wind.

Oh, to that precombustion age, when you could plan and plan but nature would decide! Oh, to those still afternoons and evenings when sailors stood on the decks of great ships, whistling for the wind as the sun set over New Jersey, amid the evening sounds, the sea hawk and the night owl. And finally the atmospheric pressure would shift, and the wind blow clean and cool and full of promise. Canvas billowed, spars creaked, a boom swung across the deck, and the ship came alive.

Reuben Keymer was on his porch when the *E. A. Johnson* sailed from Gravesend Bay on March, 20, 1860. "I felt [the wind], then saw it reach the sloop and watched the sloop going out," he told investigators. "She went southwest to clear Coney Island, then took a southerly course. I saw her three miles out to the east of Sandy Hook; the wind was west northwest; the sloop was going about eight knots an hour. . . . At the rate she was going, she would pass Sandy Hook in about an hour."

The Narrows is less open water than a tidal strait, a gateway to New York. Above it lies the Upper Bay; beyond it, the Lower Bay. In 1860 a ship moving through the Narrows would sail beside empty hills, a wilderness broken only by the occasional farmhouse. The *E. A. Johnson* passed Brighton Beach, then sailed along Staten Island.

Around midnight, Smith Watts went to the cabin to sleep. Captain Burr followed. There were four beds down there, two bunks. Oliver Watts was at the helm, steering through a seascape of dark islands. The moon went down. The stars came out. Hicks asked if he could take a turn at the wheel. As he spoke, he quietly laid an ax beside himself. He'd taken it off the pilothouse wall—it was meant for emergencies.

Oliver asked Hicks why he wanted to steer. Hicks said it was the only way he could feel calm. Oliver said okay and stepped aside. He went to the prow and stood with the wind at his back, looking out.

The men talked for a time, then Hicks seemed to notice something. Picking up the ax, he walked forward and, pointing southwest with his free hand, asked, "Is that Barnegat Light?"—meaning the lighthouse on Long Beach Island, New Jersey.

Oliver looked quickly, then said, "No. We won't see it for at least an hour."

"Look again," said Hicks. "I'm fairly certain that's Barnegat Light."

When Oliver turned that second time, Hicks swung the ax, driving it into the back of the young man's head. Oliver cried out, fell to his knees, then onto his face. In a moment, his blood was all over the deck. Hicks struck him again, just to be sure.

Oliver's brother Smith, having heard the commotion, came up the ladder and stuck his head out the cabin door. He asked Hicks what had happened. Hicks, walking with the ax behind him, pointed toward the prow and asked, "Is that Barnegat Light?" Before Smith could answer, Hicks brought the ax down onto his neck. Smith's head came off and rolled into the shadows as the body fell back into the cabin. Hicks later said decapitating Smith Watts was as easy as "cutting the trunk of a sapling tree."

Hicks went down the ladder, ax before him, hiding nothing now. Captain Burr was sitting up in bed, the headless body at his feet.

"What's happening?" asked the captain, confused.

"I think I see Barnegat Light," said Hicks.

"You won't see it for two hours," said Burr, who, getting to his feet, pushed Hicks into a wall. What followed was a three- or four-minute fight that seemingly went on for hours, as if time itself had slowed. They gripped each other, grappled and grunted and cursed as they smashed into every surface in the cabin. Hicks's main objective was to get free and swing the ax. At several points, he swung and missed—catching the blade in the wall, in the ceiling. When Captain Burr fell back onto the bed, Hicks drove the ax into the mattress. Burr got Hicks on the floor and had his hands around his neck, but Hicks was too strong. He rolled away and stood. Burr grabbed Hicks by that monkey coat. Hicks threw him off, and suddenly there was the space. He managed a good clean hard swing. "The blow took away half his head," Hicks said later. "Half his eye was on the blade, a piece of his nose and some beard."

The cabin was a mess, everything overturned, blood on the walls, blood on the floor. Hicks was spent from the effort—it was a much closer thing than he'd expected. For a moment, he thought he would be sick. He raced up the ladder, ax in hand. He stood on the deck, head down. Then just as he began to calm down, he saw something at the edge of his vision, on the periphery, where threats materialize. Oliver Watts, ax wounds in his head and back, had gotten to his feet and was coming at Hicks slowly, like a corpse, arms raised, reaching out for his killer.

Hicks stood frozen. For the first time in years, he was afraid. *What is this, man or apparition?* Hicks waited until the dying man was close, then swung the ax. Oliver Watts groaned and staggered. Grabbing hold with both hands, Hicks pushed him across the deck and threw him over the side. Yet somehow Watts, as he was falling, caught the rail and hung on, ocean zooming beneath. Hicks tried to pry loose the fingers but couldn't—there's nothing like a death grip. Hicks took a step back and brought down the ax, severing fingers and thumb, sending the dead man tumbling into the sea.

Hicks went back to the cabin, stepping over the two bodies, then stood in the pantry. He got out a mug and filled it with beer, the pale ale that seamen drank. When he finished, he refilled his mug, drank it down, then filled it again. He knocked back five or six pints in hope of recovering his equilibrium. Then he went on deck and stood looking out at Staten Island.

Why had he killed everyone on the ship if money was his object?

Because, he later explained, "Dead men tell no tales."

Hicks did not coin this phrase—it had been familiar in the criminal world since the early 1800s—but he knew it and understood what it meant: freedom.

"My bloody work was done, [and] I was alone," he went on. "No eye had seen me, and now I was free to reap the reward."

Hicks had devised a plan in his first hours among the crew. It followed a methodology he'd executed without mishap many times before. He would turn the ship around, sail through the Narrows and the Upper Bay, follow the North River above Fourteenth Street, gather all the money and finery from the lockboxes, burn the ship— "fire her"—and then escape in the yawl, vanishing into the slums of the city. The dead would be lost at the bottom of the river, on the far side of the harbor, leaving nothing to connect Hicks to the crime—he'd shipped under an alias—which would not even be considered a crime but one of those mysterious mishaps not uncommon in a life at sea.

But Hicks had more trouble handling the sloop than he had counted on. "I came near running her on the Dog Beacon, abreast of Coney Island and Staten Island lighthouse," he later said. Then just as he was regaining control, he collided with the *J. R. Mather*. "It carried away my bowsprit and brought down my foresail," Hicks said later—so much for the planned getaway.

After calling out for a time, the captain of the *Mather* sailed back toward the city, but Hicks knew it would not be long before Harbor Patrol came out to investigate. That was when he made the fatal switch to panicked contingency: *Get as much as you can as fast as you can, hide the evidence, sink the ship, and run like hell.*

He went to the cabin and roped the two bodies—the intact body of Captain Burr, and the headless body of Smith Watts—pulled them up the ladder, and tossed them over. He ransacked the cabin, smashing open boxes and trunks, rifling duffels, loading everything into the shot bag where the captain stored the cash, which Hicks did not count—no time. He searched the deck for the severed head of Smith Watts. It was dark, and it had rolled into the shadows. Hicks lost valuable minutes feeling around for it. He held it up when he found it—the sandy hair, the bloodshot eyes open, staring in disbelief. Mystics say the last image seen by a man is what he carries into the next world. Hicks tossed the head, shuddered, then tossed the ax. He retrieved an augur he'd left heating in the stove and used it to burn three holes into the cabin wall— enough, he wrongly believed, to sink the ship. He threw the shot bag into the yawl, climbed in after it, and lowered himself into the sea.

THE SHORE LINE

The news of the killings swept New York. It was, for days, a lead story in every newspaper, morning, after-noon, and evening editions, a flood of murder prose that found purest expression in the penny press, papers that could be had for next to nothing on every street corner. The *Herald,* the *Sun,* the *Gazette,* the *Mirror,* the *Daily Eagle*—these broadsheets and tabloids established the tone and the pace of the story. Beneath banner headlines— MURDER SLOOP HAUNTS CITY, GHOST SHIP HORROR—the articles turned Albert Hicks, who began as a question mark, into a celebrity: Not just a criminal or killer but the worst criminal and the bloodiest killer. Not just a bad man but, as Hicks himself later said, "the worst man who ever lived."

Unfolding crime stories tend to be owned by a single newspaper, the first to figure it out and get it right. In the case of the "Sloop Murders," a story that was, in its time, as big as the story of Al Capone or O. J. Simpson, that would turn out to be the *New York Times.* The paper had been around for less than a decade at the time of the killings. It had been founded in 1851 by the banker George Jones and the journalist-politician Henry Jarvis Raymond, who served as its inaugural editor. It started as the *New-York Daily Times,* which was shortened to the *New-York Times* in 1857. The hyphen would be dropped in 1861. The paper would not be acquired by its current ownership until 1896, when Adolph Ochs, who began as an office boy at the *Knoxville Chronicle,* picked it off the bankruptcy heap for $75,000. Its current publisher, A. G. Sulzberger, is a sixth-generation descendant of that Knoxville office boy.

In its early years, when the print market was as vibrantly wild as the Internet is today, the *Times* made its reputation in a classic manner: crime reporting. If it bled, it led. The Hicks case—the murders, the manhunt, and the trial—would be one of the stories that turned the *New York Times* into the paper of record.

You can largely credit the work of a single reporter, Elias Smith, who'd been with the paper only a short time when the *E. A. Johnson* was towed into South Street. Smith had been knocking around before that, working in single-tavern towns, chasing rumors. He had a gift for dialogue and a taste for action. He was fearless and willing not just to report but to become part of the story. He was like a weatherman who, on a blue-sky day, can make it rain.

No one knows what Elias Smith looked like. He imprinted his voice and style on the *Times* in its early years, but he left no pictures. You might imagine him with a military bearing, if only because he enlisted in the army during the Civil War and was attached to the staff of General Ambrose Burnside, but he never quit reporting. He filed regular dispatches from the front. He was at the siege of Vicksburg, where he described the Confederate soldiers as "cowardly miscreants."

Smith wrote about everything for the paper, but he was especially interested in skulduggery. Crime was the best beat because crime had everything—action, heartbreak, misery; good guys and bad guys; complicated characters with complex backstories; the built-in tension of a plot, which is just time expressed in an unusual way. A crime without a suspect is the riddle of creation. Solving it is like answering fundamental questions. A crime is the human condition boiled down to particulars. If told well, it will be the story of a certain act committed on a certain day but also the story of all mankind. It will include people and places, buildings and cops, fog-choked alleys, fugitives in flight, do-gooders and detectives in search of promotion. Every crime is a civic issue and a public interest but also personal in a way that feels like none of your goddamn business. It offers pleasure to the voyeur and to the stool pigeon. A good crime story will touch on motive, which can never be fully understood. Even when you know, you don't know.

Better still, crime stories sold newspapers. Write them well, a reporter became famous. This had partly to do with the condition of New York City. Crime seemed important in the spring of 1860, because New York City was then in the midst of the worst crime wave it would ever know. The murder rate was four times what it is today. In 2018 the murder rate was 3.4 per 100,000 people; in 1860 it was 14 per 100,000. One hundred and ten killings were reported that year, but the actual number was probably much higher—the police tended to avoid neighborhoods like the Five Points altogether, leaving homicides there unreported. The killings were blamed on the immigrants flooding the downtown streets, the unknowable slums, the gap between rich and poor, uptown and downtown, or maybe it was the police department, understaffed and corrupt. Every morning more bodies turned up, followed by stories in the penny press. And yet this particular crime—the ghost ship, its decks washed in blood—garnered special attention. The public was riveted for months. Unfolding in the summer before the Civil War, the details of the sloop murders, the uncanny wandering of that abandoned ship, seemed to catch the anxiety of a town on the edge of nervous collapse.

What was it about this crime?

It started with the victims. This wasn't a case, like so many on the waterfront, of gangsters killing gangsters, nor a case of the immigrant Irish getting slaughtered and dumped in the Five Points. These were sailors in a city of sailors, a maritime city on a maritime afternoon, murdered, along with their captain, while going about their mundane business in the Lower Bay. The Watts brothers. Captain Burr. It could have been anyone. When it could have been anyone, it is everyone. The author of such crimes has to be found and punished, the motive explained. Until then you will be driven by the sort of anxiety that makes you pick up a newspaper morning, noon, and night. You'll be like a machine stuck in high gear, looking for an answer that lets you settle back into a comfortable hum. That's what people mean when they say a body cries out for vengeance—until the killer is found, no one will be able to forget.

Then there was the nature of the crime, the gruesome violence. It was a dream that seeped into daytime. And of course the mystery—four fingers and a thumb. *Who did this?* Everyone had a theory. Maybe it had been the work of river pirates, a bloodthirsty gang out of the Fourth Ward, the Daybreak Boys or the Swamp Angels. Maybe it had been the work of the captain, driven mad by the nearness of the moon. Maybe it had been the work of a shanghaied sailor. It was only a matter of time till one of the crimps marked the wrong man, the one-in-a-million killer who would take back his freedom with a blade.

As soon as the *E. A. Johnson* was anchored at South Street, beside the Fulton Fish Market, the police began to identify its crew and search for friends and acquaintances who could vouch for each man. For the most part, this was not hard, as Captain Burr, Oliver Watts, and Smith Watts were well known on the waterfront. That was not the case with the fourth man. In fact, the more information the police gathered about him, the less they seemed to know. At first they took him to be a common sailor, one of the thousands who crowded the docks, waiting for a ship. But few people could remember much about him. He'd been seen in the presence of Captain Burr and Smith Watts, a brooding sailor in a Kossuth hat, polite but with an aura—a bad business, Reuben Keymer told police. He was listed on the manifest as William Johnson, but there was no other record of a William Johnson. In fact, the only thing the police knew for sure about William Johnson was that he was not named William Johnson.

Hart Weed was a police captain in Manhattan's second precinct, which covered everything east of Broadway between Liberty Street and Spring Street. He opened the investigation with a single lead: the missing yawl that had once hung off the back of the sloop.

Find it—that was where the trail began.

Harbor Patrol was tasked with searching for the yawl in the Upper and Lower Bay. Established in 1858, Harbor Patrol, which had started with two sergeants, twenty-five men, and five boats, was meant to battle the river pirates who ran amok on the waterfront. Its distinctive black launches were as purposeful as Roman galleys, the officers at the oars, skimming the water in long blue parkas. The patrol added a steamship later—there were tremendous battles, victories at sea—but in the early years the officers were merely trying to prove their worth. They'd had skirmishes with the Daybreak Boys and the Hookers, but the river pirates had an otherworldly ability to fade into the mist. You closed your hand around them, but when you opened it, they were gone.

Harbor Patrol searched the coasts of Brooklyn and New Jersey before finding the yawl on Staten Island, not far from Fort Tompkins on the harbor side. It had been dragged ashore and stashed in the tall grass. The beach was rocky and desolate there, climbing to farm fields, a red house in the distance. The men of Harbor Patrol stood over the yawl, examining it. There was an inch of water sloshing around the bottom, two oars, a broken tiller, what looked like half a broom handle, and a boot.

Walking into the fields, the officers located the trail and got the distinct impression that it continued inland, which was outside their jurisdiction.

They reported these findings to Captain Weed at the station house. Considering the brutality of the crime and the growing list of confusing clues—the broken bowsprit, the severed fingers—Hart Weed decided this spreading stain of a case was beyond his abilities and called in the detectives.

George Nevins must have been following the reports in the press, as transfixed as everyone else. He was one of a few dozen detectives in the police department, but he was unique. Most of the others were the kind of men a dramatist would cast in the role of detective, squarely built and handsome—their appearance alone would settle a hysterical widow. Not many crimes were solvable in those antebellum days. There was no photography, no fingerprinting, no little plastic bags, no DNA evidence. If

a killer wasn't caught in the act, if he slipped away, changed clothes, and got into a crowd, it would be nearly impossible to connect him to the crime scene. At that time, over 50 percent of all New York murder cases ended in acquittal. It was just so hard to construct a chain of evidence that linked a man to an event. The detective was a ceremonial figure as a result, a necessary part of the process—someone to go around, hear out the families, write up the report, and file it away. A detective made less money than a beat cop for this piecemeal work: three to ten dollars a day, small potatoes even in 1860. It made these men notoriously corruptible. Most had something else on the side. You could hire a New York detective to work private security. You could pay him to lose a weapon in the river, forget a fact, or walk away. Their services were advertised in the evening papers: "piping," "shadowing," "working up"—trained professional detection, ten dollars a day.

Detective Nevins was different. He looked like a beaver, short and thick, with rusty hair, a twitchy nose, and sharp eyes, and he worked and behaved like one— persistent and industrious, even dogged. He was a man of science. He believed everyone left a trail as they made their way through the world. You just needed to know how to look. If Nevins was incorruptible, it was because his horizon stretched farther. Most detectives thought about this season or next year, but Nevins was fixated on the future, when he hoped the art of investigation would become a trade. His mission was partly to protect the city and the public and partly to demonstrate the worth of his profession, which was as much a philosophy as a career.

He believed that the past could be understood, that crimes could be solved, and that fugitives could be identified and brought to justice.

Nevins, in his thirties, was a native of New York, which made him a kind of foreigner. The city had changed so much since he was a boy—the past was another country. Much of Manhattan had been a forested Eden back then, wild terrain, but it had since been remade by industry. His once-green island was now covered in cobblestone and brick. The old rim-a-rack piers had given way to tremendous wharves. Along rivers where once he'd fished for sturgeon, factories stood. The morning sky was filled with steam and smoke.

Nevins had a partner, but little is known about him. That's always the way it is—when one man leaves a deep impression, the other fades.

Soon after the yawl was found, the detectives headed to Staten Island. They went by ferry, then hired a carriage—a few were always waiting at the terminal—that took them to the shore. They got out and walked through the sand in their heavy black shoes, overcoats trailing in the bog grass. They stood around the yawl, talking. They'd brought a third man, Elias Smith of the *Times*. Everyone has a talent, and Smith's was even more important in his line than writing: he had a brilliant knack for getting himself into the center of the action. As he watched the detectives work, he offered theories of his own. It's from Elias Smith that we know many of the details of the manhunt.

Someone must have seen something. The detectives went in search of witnesses. They spent the rest of the morning going from farmhouse to farmhouse, knocking on doors, calling to people working in the fields. Staten Island was a wilderness then, its villages clustered between vast estates, crescent-shaped beaches, and tumble-down forts and walls. Ancient machinery rotted in the cattails. They found a man who had seen the yawl come ashore. In court, they would call him a "hostler," one who cares for horses. He operated a stable near the Narrows, "hard bestride Fort Tompkins." He said he'd watched a man drag a little boat up the beach, a man who "seemed nervous and restless."

The detectives found another witness, George Nedlinger, a German-born farmer who had actually spoken to the fugitive. "I saw him pass at about 6 o'clock on Wednesday morning," Nedlinger said. "He was about two hundred yards off, coming towards me, and had a big bag on his shoulder. As he came up he bade me good morning, and asked if anyone would interfere with his boat while he was away, as he had left it at the fort; I said no, and he went along; it was afterwards hauled up by some boys; when I saw him, his whiskers were rather long, and he wore a rather bluish coat, which they call a monkey-jacket, and rather a flat hat, that was squeezed down by the bag."

From that point, the killer's trail was like a neon-lit road—all the detectives had to do was follow it. Nedlinger sent them on to another witness, Michael Durney, a farmer. They caught up with him on a broad causeway that crossed the island. Durney, fussing with a mule, wanted to know more about the fugitive before he talked.

His name is William Johnson, Nevins explained. *He'd come off a boat and is wanted for questioning in a crime.*

Durney said he'd seen the man. "He was dressed in a

blue monkey-jacket, pants, and a black colored hat, and had a bag on his shoulder; he was pretty near Fort Richmond and going towards the ferry, and bid me good morning. He spoke about a boat he had left at the Fort and an oyster sloop. I did not understand him precisely; but said it was all right."

Nevins asked where the man had gone. Durney pointed up the road to Vanderbilt's ferry landing, about two miles away. The detectives and the reporter walked the distance, sun beating down on them, fields desolate in the early spring. The smell of black earth, salt in the sea wind. As they went, they looked for clues, wanting not just to see but to experience everything the man in flight had experienced: houses and cart paths, rutted country lanes.

They were footsore by the time they reached the landing.

What time does that make it? asked Nevins.

His partner checked his watch. *Noon.*

So it took us two hours?

Just under.

The ferry terminal consisted of a pier and a few ramshackle houses, with a ticket office and a newsstand. Nevins asked around till he found Abram Egbert, the dock keeper, a little German immigrant with a distinct recollection of Johnson, or Jones, or whatever they were calling him.

He came up that road just like you did, Egbert told the detectives, *only he was ragged in that monkey jacket and Kossuth hat. He was humping a big sack that looked like a shot bag and must have weighed something terrible, but he would not put it down or let it out of his sight.*

He was wild in the eyes—not nervous, more like elated. He got here just as the ferry was leaving—he missed it by two minutes. He tried to run for it, but it was no use. Once they shut the doors . . . He was not happy about that. He cursed something awful, stomped back, and asked for a ticket for the next ferry—they leave every hour. He dipped into that shot bag and pulled out a silver coin—you don't forget a ten-dollar piece. I said it was too big, and he found something smaller. He asked if there was a place to get a drink. I sent him there.

Egbert pointed to a tavern across the landing. It was the saloon of Peter Van Pelt where, according to the *Times,* the fugitive "took refreshments" and "ostentatiously displayed his money."

The detectives and the reporter sat down in the saloon and ordered coffee. They asked if anyone remembered a man who'd come in carrying a shot bag and wearing a Kossuth hat.

"Yeah, I seen him," said the bartender.

Nevins asked the bartender his name. It was Augustus Gisler. He was seventeen years old and worked in the saloon part-time, mostly mornings. It was usually the same customers every day, he said, going back and forth on the ferry, so you noticed strangers. And this man . . . with that shot bag . . . he sat down slowly, ordering a whiskey, but as soon as the liquor was in him, you could see the effect. His eyes lit up and he grinned and hefted that big sack and asked for more drinks—this time for everyone in the place. "At one point," the bartender said, "he took a gold piece out of his bag and held it to the light, then showed it to me and said, 'Hey boy, I bet you want this?' "

"I said, 'No, sir. I can't make change for that.' "

He grinned and reached into the bag for a few shillings, which he rolled across the bar. He was dark and twinkling, on a jag. He ordered breakfast—eggs and oysters. It was a spectacle, the way he wolfed down the food and piled up the shells, roaring with laughter and slapping the bar as he ordered whiskey after whiskey.

He called to Egbert, who was watching from the doorway. "Hey friend, join me for a drink before the ferry arrives."

Abram Egbert asked the stranger "if he was a seafaring man."

The fugitive then told a fantastic tale, possibly working up a cover story to explain all that money, all that burning energy. Yes, he was indeed a seafaring man, he said. He'd been the captain of a sloop that experienced bad luck in the Lower Bay, the worst kind of bad luck, the kind that makes you appreciate each moment left in your life. He'd been sailing in the Lower Bay when, in the dead of night, he'd been run into by a ship that quickly and callously sailed away. One of his crewmen had been killed, pinned by a bowsprit against the mast, and another had been knocked over—presumably he died too. He himself had been downstairs asleep at the time and only had time to get his clothes and "needful"—he shook the seabag—and get ashore in the yawl.

Are you sure that other man drowned? Egbert asked. Maybe we should alert Harbor Patrol. Maybe he's been knocked silly and is wandering around some beach.

The fugitive cut Egbert short, saying only that he was certain the man was dead.

———

The detectives and the reporter boarded the same ferry the fugitive had taken—the *Southfield,* a 750-ton side-wheel steamer that had been built in the Brooklyn Navy Yard in 1857. Refashioned as a gunboat, the *Southfield* would be lost in the Civil War, sunk by a Confederate ironclad in April 1864. It was a massive ship, filled with club rooms and galleries, the upper deck shadowed by a huge funnel, the current all around it beaten to white water.

A few days earlier, Hicks had boarded at seven A.M. The detectives and the reporter boarded in the afternoon, for a trip that felt like an Atlantic crossing. The coast of bucolic Staten Island, home to Lenape Indians and Dutch settlements, was still nearly as virgin as when Henry Hudson sailed the Narrows. From there the ferry would take them in under thirty minutes to the bustling, crime-ridden, commerce-drunk port of Manhattan.

The detectives interviewed several people on the ferry, including the captain and the steward, before finding someone who'd spoken to Hicks that morning. They were constructing a chain, searching for witnesses who, taken together, could describe every step the fugitive took on his getaway. If they missed a single link, the chain would fall apart, and the killer would slip away.

His name was Francis McCaffrey, an Irish immigrant in his early twenties. He'd arrived in America two years before, part of the great famine-driven migration. Between 1845 and 1852, 1.5 million Irish emigrated to the United States and went on to build new lives in Boston, Baltimore, Philadelphia, Buffalo, and New York. You could hear their accents, that lilting singsong, on every downtown street. On the *Southfield,* McCaffrey was a cabin boy, paid a few dollars a day to sweep floors, direct passengers, and empty ashtrays and spittoons—it was a world of tobacco juice. He told Detective Nevins that he'd noticed the fugitive, sitting by himself in an empty gallery, because of the coat. "It was patches all over," McCaffrey said. "And he had that big bag and was sitting in the ladies' cabin with his head resting on his hand."

Hicks was ragged, with dark circles under his eyes. The evening before, he'd been amid the crew of the *E. A. Johnson,* anchored in Gravesend Bay, awaiting the wind. He'd killed three people since, decapitated, brawled, suffered a collision, escaped in a yawl, rowed several miles, walked two miles across Staten Island, and consumed six glasses of ale and an entire bottle of whiskey. He'd been going this way for more than twenty-four hours.

McCaffrey had been sweeping the hallway when Hicks called him over and asked him something, but he talked so slurry and fast, it was hard to understand. "He said he was afraid fellows had been cheating him," McCaffrey told the detectives, "and asked if I was a good judge of this country's money."

U.S. currency was not entirely uniform in 1860. Various banks offered various sorts of bills. Add to that the foreign money that was floating around New York, and you had a confusing hodgepodge.

"I said I knew the gold and silver," McCaffrey said, "but did not know much about the bills. He put his hand into the bag and pulled out about six dollars silver in quarters and half-dollars, he asked me to count.

"He then asked for the water-closet, and requested of me if I would not show it to him," McCaffrey continued. "I asked him, in going along, if he would not give me the price of my bitters. When we landed at Whitehall, he came up to me and gave me a quarter and asked me to have a drink; that was all the conversation I had with him; as he was sitting in the cabin, while we were passing over, I went by him two or three times, and found him with his head on the bag, as if he were tired and resting; he had a rather dusty, crushed-looking hat on and this old monkey-jacket."

On the Manhattan side, Detective Nevins found a man who had spoken to Hicks at the Whitehall Street Landing. Charles La Coste operated a news and snack stand at the corner of Broadway and Stage Terminal. He said Hicks had asked for coffee and a piece of cake. La Coste had watched him wolf it down. The fugitive had the feral look of a forest animal that finds itself in town, fascinatingly alive, mesmerizing but scary.

That'll be six cents, La Coste had said. Hicks handed over a gold coin.

La Coste said he couldn't make change for it—ten dollars was more than he saw in a half day. "[Hicks] rooted around in the bag and came out with two shillings and a cent," La Coste told the detectives.

Hicks then asked La Coste if he knew where he could hire a hack, a horse-drawn taxi. La Coste said it was still too early—there'd be no hacks for a few hours. He suggested Hicks catch the East Broadway stage.

Hicks would have felt his tremendous weariness then. He was only a mile from home, but the thought of setting out on another long walk, with the heavy bag on his shoulder and booze and coffee in his system, in his scattered state of mind . . . when you closed your eyes, you saw and felt it all again . . . the faces of Captain Burr and the Watts brothers, the glint of the ax, the struggle, searching for the head in the dark, how easily it had come off, like a sapling. . . . Hicks had to sit down, shut the door, and be alone in the dark with the seabag for two or three hours.

He asked La Coste if there was a hotel nearby, a flop where he could be alone before he went back to his wife and child. La Coste suggested the respectable sort of place—French's Hotel—that was exactly wrong for Hicks.

The fugitive, flashing coins and hugging that sack, had attracted the attention of street hawkers, riffraff. A bootblack asked Hicks if he wanted a shine. Hicks looked at his boots—studied them carefully, as if seeing for the first time their cracked leather, tarnished buckles, and worn-out soles. They'd walked a thousand miles, had a thousand more to go. Hicks seemed to consider it—he was rich now, wasn't he?—then changed his mind, saying something like *Nah, these shoes ain't worth a shilling.*

Kids gathered around him, wastrels—ten-, twelve-, fifteen-year-old boys who'd wandered over from the Five Points and adjacent slums, ragamuffins looking for a dollar. They were dark-eyed and ratty in their cast-off clothes, worn till they rotted and fell free. They lived outside in the sun, as natural a part of the environment as the gulls that lit on the rooftops. Hicks eyed the boys warily. A cop can be fooled, but a child sees right through you.

La Coste, as he was telling his story to Detective Nevins, pointed out the same kids. They were standing in a pack, watching at a distance. Nevins called them over and introduced himself, then asked if any of them remembered the man with the seabag. They all did. Could any of them describe him in detail?

A boy stepped forward, sixteen-year-old William Drumm, bigger than the others. He said he lived at 8½ Stone Street. Today Stone Street is in the heart of Manhattan's financial district, shadowed by glass and steel towers, but back then it was a rickety lane. One of the shortest and oldest blocks in the city, it was home to the continent's first brewery—built by the Dutch West India Company in 1632—a headwater of the torrent of ale that still floats the metropolis.

Drumm occasionally worked for La Coste but mostly just hung around, waiting for incoming ferries, selling his services to travelers. "I offered to carry his bag," he explained, because he looked so tired and so clearly had a long way to go. Hicks accepted the offer with relief. Drumm hoisted the sack—it was much heavier than he'd expected, it "cut deeply into my shoulder," he told the detectives—then headed out behind the fugitive, who set a brisk pace.

Nevins asked Drumm what route he'd taken with Hicks. He wanted to trace the path, see if he could make sense of it. The little party followed State Street across Bowling Green, then walked up Broadway, which had once been an Indian trail. Before the Civil War, you could still see evidence of that, in the hard-packed dirt, in the way it rambled, and in the smells, which were the smells of America old and new, smells of horse manure and leather and human sweat, but also the stench of factories; of putrid meat from the slaughter yards and tanneries, of oil from the gasworks and refineries. A decade later the city would actually produce a stench map, which people consulted in determining which parts of the city to avoid. Because a bad smell can ruin your day.

It had still been early morning when William Drumm followed Albert Hicks. The city had been deserted. There had been smoke and steam. Foghorns moaned as big ships passed behind buildings at the end of every street. Now it was afternoon, crowded. The detectives, the reporter, and the boy had to maneuver through hustling merchants who pushed carts of product, businessmen returning from lunch to the trading houses, garment workers bound for sweatshops and mills. Clothing stores, feed shops, dry goods stores—alleys, apartments, redbrick and mansard roofs, stoops and clapboard houses that would not have looked out of place on the frontier, churches, tenements, firetraps with empty windows, the laundry strung above the weedy, trash-choked yards.

The detectives asked Drumm how the fugitive had carried himself, looked, behaved. Was he nervous? Excited? What had he said?

The man had said nothing, Drumm told them, just went on and on, dead-eyed, in a trance. "We went about a mile, then stopped here."

They were standing at the corner of Cedar and Greenwich streets, amid horse traffic and foot traffic—the layout of the streets has been changed, but the intersection would look familiar to anyone who has rambled around Lower Manhattan. It was already among the most densely populated parts of the city. How simple it would be for a man to lose himself in such chaos.

"What then?" asked Nevins.

"He took the bag from my shoulder, and asked how much I expected to be paid," Drumm said.

The boy wanted what would be about five dollars

today; he'd seen Hicks waving around that gold coin. A man going past called out to Hicks, "That boy is trying to rob you. Bag hauling is two shillings."

Hicks had looked at Drumm severely, as if reassessing, reached into his sack, and counted out three shillings, about ninety cents today. Drumm protested—he'd carried that heavy bag a long way. That's all you're getting, said Hicks. "Now get, or I'll kick you."

The detectives spent the rest of the day trying to figure out where Hicks had gone from there. They knocked on doors and talked to merchants and vendors, but New York is really a series of small towns. A man familiar on one block will be unknown on the next. In this manner, the link was lost and the chain fell apart.

Nevins returned to the precinct in despair. In those days, in the absence of the tools available to modern investigators, such a failure usually meant the end of a chase.

The next morning a stranger showed up at the precinct house, looking for Detective Nevins. His name was Burke, and he operated an apple stand on Greenwich Street. He also managed the apartment house at 129 Cedar, three blocks from the North River, collecting rents, making repairs, working as a sort of superintendent. He knew every tenant in the building, among whom, he believed, was the person responsible for the murders on the *E. A. Johnson.*

The man lived with his wife and small child, Burke said to Detective Nevins. He had gone to sea a week before, telling his wife he'd be away a month, but he had returned weeks ahead of schedule stuffed with cash—

coins and bills spilling from his pockets. He handed out shillings like candy. Asked how he'd come into this windfall, he'd told a fantastic story: part of it had come from an unexpected inheritance, a distant relative with no close kin, and part had come from good luck—he'd found a ship abandoned in the bay and sold it for scrap. The story kept changing.

Nevins asked Burke for more details: What did the man look like? How old was he, and how big? How did he behave? Burke guessed his age, height, and weight, then described him as not unkind. "He's been in the building close to three years and always paid on time," said Burke. "He always paid me my rent like an honest man."

"Where are they now?" asked Nevins, meaning the man and his family.

"Gone," said Burke. "Packed up everything and rushed out."

Nevins accompanied Burke to 129 Cedar Street, a wooden tenement a block from where Hicks had paid Drumm three shillings for carrying his sack. Cedar Street looked then as it looks today—short and narrow, the sky shut out, walls closing in. The tenement has been replaced by a brick tower that sits beside O'Hara's Pub a block west of Zuccotti Park. A two-bedroom apartment on Cedar Street currently goes for around $4,500 a month. Hicks had paid five bucks for a bedroom and space for the child. No bath, nor running water—just a woodstove, grim walls, and refracted light.

It's not clear if Nevins got a search warrant or would have needed to—he was in hot pursuit of a killer. Burke had a key to the apartment. The detective walked through the rooms slowly, examining. If you narrow your focus, it's surprising how much you can perceive. The less you look at, the more you see. The rooms had been cleaned out. Closets, drawers, shelves were all empty. Bits of paper and trash were scattered here and there. Debris. Clues. One of them turned out to be important: a tarnished silver compass, its crystal cracked but the needle still shivering as it swung around to point north. It connected the tenant of the house—or former tenant—to the waterfront.

The detectives, having recovered the trail, spent the rest of the morning canvassing the nearby streets: Greenwich, Thames, Trinity. More than a few merchants remembered Hicks, especially as he had been that day. "He'd swaggered about the neighborhood, seemingly seeking notoriety, asking everyone with whom he could claim the shadow of an acquaintance to drink," the *Times* reported. "In the course of the day, he purchased $40 worth of clothing from a secondhand dealer in Greenwich Street. One man asserts that he was curious to know where [Hicks] had obtained his sudden wealth, and was told by the fugitive, in reply to questions, that the vessel on which he had shipped had been sold, and the money in question was his share of the proceeds."

Nevins knew that Hicks must have traded his mishmash of loot for a uniform currency—he must have laundered the cash. He inquired in a half-dozen exchanges before he found the broker, Albert James, an officer at the Farmers' & Citizens' Bank of Williamsburg, 116 South Street, Manhattan. The house accepted trades: you brought in a mess of coins and paper, and an officer determined its worth, then gave you a stack of notes unique to that bank. James had indeed dealt with a man like the one described by Nevins. The banker remembered the encounter well—the man's rough hands and demeanor, how he emptied the big seabag onto the desk, the racket the coins made. The broker said he'd been suspicious right away; the man had been gleeful and smelled of liquor.

A merchant house had recently been robbed; thieves had gotten away with stolen silver. "Is this part of that?" the broker had asked Hicks.

"No, sir."

"Tell the truth, sailor boy. Are you mixed up with that business?"

"No, sir. I've come by this money honestly."

"How?" asked the banker.

Hicks told yet another story: a sick sea captain, bedridden in a foreign port, had sent his mate to New York with bills and coins to exchange for clean money that could be used to hire a doctor. "I am my captain's only hope," Hicks told the broker. "How much will you give me?"

The broker did some figuring: "$260," he said. "$130 for the silver. $130 for the gold."

Hicks agreed. When he got the fresh bills, he shoved them into his sack and left.

Everyone Nevins talked to painted the same picture of the fugitive—a man eager to spend his money, swanning up and down the avenue, elated and wild, maintaining a steady state of inebriation, as free with information as he was with cash. He told a dozen stories about how he'd come into his fortune, and a dozen more about what he'd do with it. He was consistent with just one detail: where he'd go next. He was headed up the coast, he said, possibly to Stonington, Connecticut, possibly to Providence, Rhode Island. He planned to take the *Common-wealth,* a big ferry that stopped at several ports on Long Island Sound.

Why was Albert Hicks, aka William Johnson, so incautious? Why did he shoot his mouth off like the drunken sailor he was?

Because he believed he'd already gotten away with it. He'd sunk the ship and left the bodies at the bottom of the harbor. No bodies meant no evidence; no evidence meant no crime. Being followed . . . being chased . . . getting caught . . . it never even occurred to him.

The detectives traveled to Stonington by train—the Shore Line's tracks hugged the New England coast from New York all the way to Massachusetts. Owned by the New York, Providence & Boston Railroad, the service had been operating since 1838. The coaches were large and roomy, elegant in the way of old-leather America, brandy, cigar smoke, and brass spittoons. From the window, Nevins watched the countryside go by—fishing villages and farms, shingle-roof houses and bay front meadows.

Nevins had brought along *Times* reporter Elias Smith. Even then, the term *embedded* was used, as for a tick or a leech. Smith had sold himself to the detectives as a resource: having grown up near Providence and Stonington, he knew the streets and wharves. The two cities were forty-five miles apart as the crow flies, four hours by train—the detectives would drag the fields and towns in between the way schooner captains dragged the Grand Banks. "Being familiar with the description given of the supposed murderer, and, withal, fully posted upon the general locale of places and routes in Rhode Island, your reporter was deputized to accompany the officers as a guide and assistant," Smith reported on March 23, 1860.

At six P.M. the train arrived in Stonington, a hub on Long Island Sound, a pass-through to every kind of schooner and sloop. The detectives and the reporter went straight to the ferry terminal, where the *Commonwealth*— the ship Hicks told people he would take—landed twice a day. There it sat among workaday boats like a prince among peasants, tall and grand, its decks gleaming in the setting sun. Passengers were disembarking when Nevins walked up. He showed his badge to a steward. *New York City police. We need to see the clerk.*

The head clerk, Foster, was summoned. Nevins explained the situation: *We are on the trail of a dangerous fugitive. We have reason to believe he's been on your ship.* Nevins identified the wanted man as "William Johnson, sometimes goes by Bill." He did not have a photo or sketch, but he gave a description based on what he'd been told by witnesses: a big man, forty years old, with a dark beard and dark eyes. He was said to be traveling with a woman and a child.

Maybe it was mentioning the beard that did the trick, or maybe it was the fugitive's furtive air, but Foster did indeed remember such a man, or thought he did. The clerk went into the records office to check the manifest and came back grinning. He showed Nevins the entry— *There's the name, right there.* "W. Johnson. Mr., Mrs., Child." Why Hicks would continue to use his alias even as he made his getaway is a bit of mystery. Perhaps he was more comfortable traveling under an assumed identity, or perhaps he'd let confidence get the better of common sense. "They'd checked bags," Foster said. "A suitcase and a duffel."

According to the manifest, Johnson and family continued from Stonington to one of the towns up the Mystic River. That meant they took a river ferry, Foster explained—a hired ship that traveled from village to village.

The detectives and the reporter walked to the charter terminal as the sun sank, casting long shadows on inky water. Nevins found a captain who indeed remembered someone like the wanted man—woman, child. *See . . . in the book . . . the names.* Nevins hired the same ferry, and the three men boarded it and headed upriver. After about two hours, they disembarked at a small town.

Nevins asked around, talking to mates and dockmasters, before he found a bag handler who remembered a William Johnson. He said he'd helped the man find lodging and even spoke to the wife and child.

"Spoke to the wife and child? How's that?" asked Nevins.

"Just like I said. We spoke."

"The child is barely more than a babe in arms," said Nevins. "He can't know more than a few words."

"Well, this warn't no babe in arms," said the bag handler. "This was an older boy, twelve at least. And impudent. A real cuss."

That was how Nevins learned he was on the wrong trail, chasing a false lead, wasting precious hours. He made it back to Stonington in the wee hours, tired and deflated. He took a room in a small waterfront hotel, awoke early, shook it off, and got back to work. He went to the train station and sent his partner to the ferry landing. The detectives questioned employees on every incoming and outgoing train and ship. *Have you seen . . . have you seen . . . have you seen . . .* When they began to meet the same porters for a second or even third time, they knew it was time to move on.

If not Stonington . . .

They went by train to Providence, arriving at night. Slept in a railroad hotel, took a businessman's breakfast in the morning—eggs, bacon, biscuits, coffee. The Rhode Island newspapers were filled with details of the killings and the chase: *Where was this monster, and what if he were never found?*

Providence was a big town on the East Coast, a raucous seaport with sailors from every part of the world—an easy place to ditch a weapon and vanish. It had been surpassed in size by Manhattan, which left behind every other city with the opening of the Erie Canal, but it was still in the running for new world metropolis—a diverse town with a mixed population of fifty thousand, natives and immigrants, its own folklore and underworld history. The city you see today, modern Providence is, in a sense, what remains of that freewheeling town. In Providence, it never got better than it was in 1860—the elegant avenues, the limestone buildings, storefronts shaded in the setting sun, the hills leading down to the waterfront gin mills, saloons, and joints.

The detectives checked the big ferries and the small ferries—those that stopped in Stonington and those that came directly from New York. Nevins was convinced the killer had come by water. He was a sailor after all, a pirate.

Nevins enlisted the help of the local authorities, particularly Detective George Billings of the Providence police department. Billings took the visitors on a tour of the dives. For the New York detectives, it would have been their world in miniature, and they would have looked down on the city and its police in the usual way of the boys from the bigger town. "We drove around the city to all the sailor-boarding houses, and to all the railroad depots, questioning baggage-masters and everyone likely to give us information, but could get no satisfactory clue," Nevins reported.

Meanwhile Elias Smith was stuck on a question: *Why are we so certain our man traveled the most well-worn route?* Pulling Nevins aside, he said, "Maybe he didn't come from New York or from Stonington."

"Then from where?"

"Maybe he took the ferry from New York to Fall River, Massachusetts," said Smith, who knew Fall River as a port, a commercial and transportation center. Fall River was like O'Hare International Airport. Given enough time, everyone ended up going through it. "Once there, he could've gotten the *Bradford Durfee*— a steamship—down river into Providence," Smith explained.

"Why would he do that?"

"To throw us off the trail."

By this point, Hicks, having seen the newspaper headlines, would've realized his attempt to sink the *E. A. Johnson* had failed—that the police had the sloop in custody.

Nevins was skeptical. The fugitive had shown no previous signs of trying to cover his tracks. Hadn't he gone up and down Greenwich Street flashing his money? Did that sound like a man who'd go ten hours out of his way to confuse police?

They argued back and forth.

"I don't buy it," Nevins said, "but if you want to check it out for yourself, go ahead."

"Leaving these officers to work up their part of the case, I struck out on my own hook," Smith reported in the *Times*. "The *Bradford Durfee* was still at the dock, and my first thought was to question her crew. The first man I spoke to was John McDermott, an intelligent deckhand. I said, 'You brought up a sailor man from Fall River, yesterday. Can you tell me what baggage he had?' John promptly replied, 'Yes,' and immediately gave a precise list of every article, adding 'he had his wife with him—a little woman, with a child, and she had weak eyes.'"

This was the first Smith had heard of Mrs. Hicks's myopia, a detail that would become important later, when she was depicted as a pathetic, pitiable innocent. Those weak eyes are one of the only things we know for certain about the killer's wife.

The fugitive had asked the deckhand if he could recommend a hotel in Providence, an out-of-the-way place "where he could go for a few weeks." The deckhand could not—he did not live here—but he sent Hicks to a cabdriver who could. Smith reported in the *Times*:

> I was now fully satisfied that I had got on the track
> of the fugitive, and the next point was to trace him
> by the hack-man who took him, his family, and the
> baggage from the boat. Though willing to give all

the information he possessed, the deckhand could not [remember] the number of the hack, nor the name of the driver, but he gave such a description of the man and of his horses as would furnish a good clue. In less than half an hour, I found the residence of the driver of the carriage, who proved to be Mr. Reuben Wyman, of Hack No. 6. He was asleep, but, on being called, promptly gave a full description of the baggage, and told where he had carried it.

The house where [Hicks] had taken lodgings is at the extreme south-east and in the least frequented part of the city, where, by observing ordinary precaution, [a person] might stay a long time without fear of discovery. The name of the lady who consented to take [him and his family] to board is Mrs. Crowell, a respectable widow.

Smith left the driver, promising he'd see him again, then went to talk to Nevins, who he found beavering around the ferry terminal, frustrated, muttering. Smith told the detective what he'd learned from the hack about the boardinghouse on the edge of Providence.

"I'm sure our man is there," Smith said.

Nevins sent an officer to pick up the driver and bring him to the Providence police station, where he answered questions. He offered to take Nevins to the boardinghouse where he'd dropped off the fugitive: "I'll show you where . . ."

The group traveled in the hack's carriage, the cobblestone streets turning to gravel, then dirt, night coming on. The driver was around thirty years old, a German immigrant with a mustache. He was uneasy and talked the whole way in his thick accent.

What's making you so nervous? asked Nevins.

The man you are looking for is not the sort of man you play with, explained the driver.

They reached the hotel at sundown. Only it wasn't a hotel. It wasn't even an inn. It was a rickety boarding-house in the fields. The porch sagged, and the upper windows were like sad eyes in a sad face. A tremendous beech tree shaded the yard, the trunk as smooth as river stone, its ribbed leaves as green as limes, with pale undersides that quaked in the wind. The tree filled like a sail on a blustery day, bellying out like the main canvas on a clipper ship. For two dollars, the cost of a steak at Delmonico's in New York, you could engage rooms in such a place for a week.

Nevins sent the driver to knock on the door and told him to ask for William Johnson. If anyone wanted to know what it was about, Nevins told the driver to say it was about counterfeit money—say that Johnson had paid his fare in phony bills. Nevins and the others, looking through drawn curtains from the back of the carriage, watched the driver talk to the mistress of the house. She heard him out, went away, then came back with a woman who, Nevins realized, was Johnson's wife. Smith had told Nevins about her myopia, but now he could see it for himself: she got right up close when she talked. Later, when Nevins wrote his report, he called her "sore-eyed," then noted her general appearance: small, delicately made.

The driver told the woman that her husband had paid in counterfeit bills. She said he had gone out but would be back. "Please be quiet if you come," she added. "There's a child sleeping."

After the driver returned to the hack and told Nevins what had happened, the detective devised a plan. Early in the morning, when the fugitive would be asleep, Nevins would return to the house with a detachment of Providence police. They'd surround the building, cutting off every getaway, then wake the suspect and confront him with the invented charge of counterfeiting. Maybe he could be tricked into a confession.

At one A.M. the countryside was deserted, and the sky awash in stars. Police surrounded the boardinghouse, and Nevins sent a local cop to the door. He banged three times. One moment turned into another, then another. Silence. "Again," said Nevins. *Bang, bang, bang!*

A window opened on the second floor. A woman stuck her head out—the proprietress. She was not happy. "What is it?"

"Police. We're here to see Mr. William Johnson."

"Why?"

"Counterfeiting. Paid a hack in bad bills. We need to clear it up."

The widow cursed as she let them in. She had not liked the look of Johnson from the start. She should have trusted her instinct, she said, and promised to never make that mistake again. She led the police to a room on the first floor.

Nevins tried the door. Open. He went in, followed by eight cops. They filled the room completely, bottom to top, casting shadows on the walls. Nevins called out: "Johnson, Johnson. William Johnson!"

The wife got up, groggy and confused. *What's this*

about? The child started to cry, first a whimper, then a scream.

Nevins told the sore-eyed woman he needed to talk to her husband. She said he was asleep in the next room.

Nevins went in and held a kerosene lamp over the bed. It was piled with blankets. He pulled them away, and there was the fugitive, stone-faced, staring ahead. At the end of the search, you find yourself puzzled. You are expecting a monster, but you find only a man. Or maybe it's something more. Maybe you are expecting God or the devil, or an answer to a fundamental question, and instead you discover yourself in a small room in a small city as a child cries.

"I woke him and he immediately began to sweat," Nevins later said. "My God, how he did sweat!"

"Get up and put on your clothes," said Nevins, standing an inch from the fugitive, staring, examining, and wondering: *Can this really be the man?*

Nevins asked the man for his name.

He hesitated, looked down, started to speak, then reconsidered. "My right and proper name is Albert W. Hicks."

"What do you mean, 'right and proper'?" asked Nevins.

"Sometimes I go by the name Johnson—that is, when I go to sea."

Nevins told the fugitive he was wanted for counterfeiting.

The man laughed.

What's funny?

"Do I look like a counterfeiter?" he said. Then: "I'm not a counterfeiter. I'm a sailor."

"Let me see your hands," said Nevins. "If you're a

sailor and not a counterfeiter, as you claim, your hands will make it clear."

Hicks raised his hands, then turned them over, showing his palms in the lamplight. They were hard and calloused, too big for his body. Once you noticed them, you could not stop noticing them.

"Do these look like the hands of a counterfeiter?" asked Hicks.

"No," said Nevins, "they don't."

Nevins asked Hicks the basic questions: *How long have you been in Providence? Where did you come from? What is your business?*

"He replied with hesitation," Smith later reported, "as if taking time to weigh the effect of his answers. He said he came from Fall River, and had not been in New York for two months."

The police searched the rooms. Trunks, sacks, cases. According to the report, the baggage "consisted of a sailor's chest, with a cotton fringed cover, a bundle of bedding, and two cotton bags filled with clothing."

"I found a silver watch," Nevins said, "since identified as Captain Burr's, also, his knife, and, among the rest, two small canvas bags, which have since been identified as those used by the Captain to carry his silver." Hicks had $121 in his pocket, most of it in bills issued by the Farmers' & Citizens' Bank of Williamsburg.

The complete contents of the search, listed in the police report, offers a glimpse of nineteenth-century seafaring life: "A silver watch, No. 21,310; a jack-knife, a brass door-key; a red silk figured handkerchief; a white silk figured do, with a blue border; a small inlaid box containing a few small articles commonly used by sailors in mending clothes and sails; a leather wallet containing a locket ring with the likeness of a lady under a carnelian seal."

That last item—"the likeness of a lady"—would prove important. It was a daguerreotype of the dark-haired girl who had been meant to marry Oliver Watts. Hicks probably didn't even know what it was—only that, in his hurry, he had wanted it. "We were also shown a signet ring . . . in the trunk of the prisoner's wife," Smith reported, "which, from its elaborate workmanship, its massiveness and careful engraving, we figured must be exceedingly valuable. It bears the motto: 'Nunquam mutare'—Never change."

Hicks was arrested, his property carried away. "I didn't take his wife's baggage," Nevins said. "I felt so bad for her that I gave her $10 out of the money. Poor woman! As it was, she cried bitterly, but if she had known what her husband was really charged with, it would have been awful."

On the way to the police station—early morning, horse hooves on paving stone, buildings ghostly at first light—Nevins asked Hicks how he had come into possession of so much money. He was, after all, a common sailor.

Hicks said he had gotten it from his brother. Then, reconsidering, he said he had made it "speculating around the market," which might sound absurd, but there had been an active stock exchange in Manhattan since 1792. It was not unknown for a workingman with a few extra dollars to trade bonds, cotton, or corn.

Hicks seemed oddly calm as he was brought to the jail. He went into a cell, lay his head on the mattress, closed his eyes, and went to sleep.

———

Detective Nevins wired New York, telling his chief that an arrest had been made. He planned to escort the fugitive back to the city early the next morning. Nevins then wrote his report, sitting at a wooden desk, now and then looking up from his work to gaze out the window at the brick chimneys and tin roofs of a coastal city, smoke rising into the sky over the harbor. Nine A.M. "In person Hicks is tall and strongly built, being about five feet ten inches in height, with a slight stoop in his shoulders," he wrote. His beard was raggedy and unkempt—what cops called a fugitive's beard. "His arms are long and sinewy, and his hands very large and much hardened by work. His complexion is dark, and he has high cheek bones, and a stout crop of straight, black hair. His eyes are black, and rather small, with an unsteady and revengeful expression. He is a native of Foster, R.I., and is 32 [sic] years of age."

Early in the morning Hicks asked for a pipe. He smoked slowly, with great concentration. After a time, Elias Smith was sent into the cell to tell the prisoner the true nature of the charges. This was unusual, having a newspaperman perform this task, but Nevins wanted to be free to study his suspect. Even the most hardened man might have a tell, a tic that betrays his guilt. We all want to be found out. If we're not caught, how can we be forgiven?

"The charge is not really counterfeit," the newspaperman told the prisoner.

"I didn't think so," said Hicks.

As Smith detailed the murder charges, Nevins studied

the prisoner's face. He could see neither a flicker nor any suggestion of shame. Hicks remained stoic throughout. "On being informed of the crime with which he was charged, he exhibited no particular surprise, but just shook his head, saying, 'I don't know nothing about it,' " Smith wrote. " 'If you have taken me up for that you've got the wrong man.' "

"He denied all knowledge of the sloop *E. A. Johnson*," Smith added later. "He said he never was in her, and did not know Captain Burr. He had never been in an oyster vessel. He was told that there were persons who could identify him . . . as the man who was on board that vessel when she left New York for Virginia."

Hicks scratched his head, yawned, and said he felt cold, but he admitted nothing.

"He was asked if he was willing to accompany the detectives back to New York to show that he was not implicated in the murder," Smith continued. "He answered promptly that he was, and after some further conversation he was handed the [extradition paper] to which he affixed his mark, for he cannot write."

The party was on the train by eight A.M., speeding south down the coast. Crowds waited at each stop, dark-hatted masses hoping to catch a glimpse of the monster who'd done those terrible things. News of the fugitive's capture had leaked and was already in the newspapers. A mob gathered at the station in Old Saybrook, Connecticut. Around five hundred were waiting in New London, where Nevins and the prisoner, who did not wear cuffs and was in no way identifiable, crossed the platform to switch trains. Captain Burr had been liked in New London, and many in the crowd, it was later said, had known the crew of the *E. A. Johnson* personally. They called out, cried for revenge. Some spat at Hicks, shouting, "There's the murderer! Lynch him—lynch him!"

Nevins told the prisoner not to worry: "I'll shoot the first man who touches you."

"Hicks manifested considerable repugnance to these attentions along the route, and finally began to show signs of fear . . . ," Nevins said later. "His mind was quieted by telling him, what appears to be fact, that half the people did not seem to know which of the party was the criminal, the police from the captive. They were as likely to lynch me as they were to lynch him."

Nevins picked up a tabloid along the way. The story of the arrest was on the front page. What a strange sensation for Nevins, to be chronicled in real time. The eye watches you watch the eye.

Nevins asked Hicks if he wanted to hear the article. Hicks shrugged. Nevins began to read: "'ALBERT W. HICKS, alias WILLIAM JOHNSON, the alleged murderer of Capt. BURR and his two townsmen on board of the sloop *E. A. Johnson,* was arrested at Providence, R.I., by the officers who went in pursuit of him from this City.'"

"[Hicks] listened nervously to every particular," Nevins said later, "turned pale at times, and showed much uneasiness."

Turning away, Hicks said, "I know nothing about it."

"You'll be identified in New York," said Nevins.

"You are free to think whatever you like," Hicks replied.

If Hicks had not been convinced of his imminent release, he might have made a run for it. He'd been known as a breakout artist. But crimes were wildly hard to prove in that era, especially murder in the absence of bodies, so he was certain he'd soon be free, so certain that he went easily, without a struggle. Being in police custody was in fact the only thing protecting him from the mob.

The train continued through Connecticut into Westchester County, then crossed the Harlem River into upper Manhattan. It was still undeveloped, the old Indian wilderness, rocky, green and blue. Now and then the cars rattled past an intersection in the woods, the corner of 108th Street and Fourth Avenue, say, laid out as if by a lunatic, an urban crossing amid sumac and pine, like a street corner in the jungle. There was no transition from country to city. The woods began a dozen feet from the last streetlight. One moment it was the primeval wilderness of James Fenimore Cooper, the next it was the opera houses and elegant squares of Edith Wharton. Below 42nd Street, the city became the city we know, stately mansions lined as if in rank, a bulwark against the everencroaching slums.

The train tracks ran down the middle of Fourth Avenue. A man was stationed at each crossing, shouting and swinging a bell, yet hundreds of people were run down each year. The smell of New York City, which was leather and woodsmoke and horses, drifted into the railcar.

The engine slowed as it crossed 30th Street, then stopped at the 27th Street station, the last stop on the line, with a tremendous squeal of breaks, the sooty carriages vanishing in a billow of steam. A crowd waited here, too. They clamored for the fugitive, demanded to see the killer. Having expected as much, Nevins had hidden Hicks beneath the sacks of mail in the baggage car. *Let the yokels look in the windows, walk through the coach—they will find nothing.* Later, after the crowd dissipated, Nevins led Hicks through the station, neither cuffs nor gun necessary. A Studley & Company horse coach waited on the avenue. The horses whinnied, the whip flashed, and off they went. The carriage wandered through the dark streets, wagons and night traffic. All those faces, all those mysterious lives.

The precinct was on Ann Street, a few blocks from the Spring Street pier, where Albert Hicks had first met Captain Burr. Life is not a circle, it's a hangman's knot.

Hicks got out of the carriage coolly, nodding at the waiting crowd. People were surprised by the fugitive, and troubled. He did not look like a killer. He was handsome. He smiled as he went by, winked as he walked up the steps between the detectives. Nevins was grinning, too, like a dog returning with a bone.

Isaiah Rynders was waiting in the station, his feet up on a desk, his arms spread in welcome. He was tall and elegant, in the best sort of suit, with steel-tipped boots and a western tie. His hair was slicked back, and his face was powdered in the way of a stage star, as perfumed as a dandy on Broadway. He knew how to play his part: the federal marshal imposing order on chaos.

He'd been following the manhunt on the wire. If the killings had happened in the Upper Bay, the case would have gone to the City of New York and its chief of police. Because they happened in the Lower Bay—federal property—it went to the U.S. marshal. He was a sharp politician who understood the value of a sensation.

What do you do if you find yourself in possession of a circus freak?

Sell tickets.

Isaiah Rynders was not unlike many of the criminals he was in charge of policing. Born in 1804 near Albany, he had made his name—first name, anyway—commanding North River sloops, trim three-sail sailboats that, on market mornings, filled the river from bank to bank. The skipper of such ships learned to battle by necessity—everything was about speed, getting there first. Rynders hauled produce from farms to harbor towns. He was soon refusing to answer to Isaiah, or even Mr. Rynders. If you wanted him, you called him Captain.

Fame came later, out west, when he worked on the Mississippi River. He had gone to the frontier for the same reason as everyone else—for adventure. His appearance was striking, dark with pale blue eyes. Kit Carson. Wyatt Earp. Billy the Kid. That was the era, and that was the energy. Everything was wide open, everyone was going to get rich. He became a notorious knife fighter. You'd see him with that big bowie, bent low, juggling it between his palms. He worked on the big river ships, sometimes as a card dealer, sometimes as a gambler, a never-to-be-trusted sharp playing with his own stake.

Faro was his game. For centuries, it had been a preferred diversion in every sort of casino and saloon. It favored psychology over skill. It was all about the bluff, reading the truth in the eyes of the other man. *And look what he's doing with his hands! And look how he twists*

that ruby pinky ring! Rynders excelled as a dealer and a player, stroking his mustache while considering. His nose was too large—you noticed it more as the years went by. His eyes were piercing. He had a birthmark below his left cheek, which called attention to the sharp bones of his face. His skull was close to the surface.

Faro made him rich and endangered his life. He was always fighting or running or being threatened. It was in these years that he became a master of human nature: he learned to spot hidden value and choose only those fights he knew he could win. It was said that he stabbed a man to death in Natchez, Mississippi, late one night on a smoky riverbank. He was chased from Vicksburg by vigilantes. He burned through the West, consuming it as a hungry person consumes a meal. He retreated and returned east. He operated a racing stable in South Carolina. He was that most beautiful thing—a dissipated young man, fearful that his best days were already behind him. He drank and slept and took bets, amassing a treasure that would let him return to New York in style.

He lost it all in the Panic of 1837. That phrase is so antique—"the Panic of '37"—that you almost love it, as is often the case with suffering seen from afar. Up close it was the bust that followed the boom, banks shuttered, businesses failing. Rynders returned to Manhattan anyway—made money at the tables, borrowed more and got to work, using all he had learned on the frontier to set himself up as a go-to guy, the man behind the man, the man who can get the thing you want but are not supposed to have.

He opened a grocery in the Five Points, then another, then another. He would eventually own seven such stores in the slum. They were called groceries but were more like groggeries, a legitimate front hiding a tavern and a gambling den in back. In this way, Isaiah Rynders came to amass first money, then power, then influence. By 1850, he sat at the head of a great army of Irish kids. He was the grown-up behind the Dead Rabbits, one of the city's most notorious street gangs. He used force to punish his enemies and help his friends. If asked to define him, newspaper reporters used the term *sport,* which is what they called downtown swells who wore parrot-colored clothes and shiny shoes, smiled with toothpicks in their mouths, haunted the taverns and billiard halls, bet on the ponies and the fights, and went everywhere in a group of connected guys, living a Sunday kind of life, never in an office but always at work.

Captain Rynders operated out of Sweeney's House of Refreshment, a lunch counter at 11 Ann Street. He later opened his own joint, the Empire Club at 25 Park Row.

He'd sit under a dim light in back, laughing and talking. *Don't worry—I'll take care of it. Forget the kraut—he's a nimenog and will be dealt with.* In short, he was a fixer, the so-called "King of the Five Points," where you'd go if you needed the Irish vote. With his crew of Dead Rabbits, he worked in the way of a modern Mafia boss. ("The brutal and turbulent ruffian who led the mob, and controlled the politics of the lower wards," was how Teddy Roosevelt described Rynders.) On Election Day, he sent his army into the streets. They were expert at turning out repeaters, those who voted early and often. He helped get out the vote for Franklin Pierce in the presidential election of 1852. It was said he secured the presidency for James Buchanan in 1856. It was President Buchanan who appointed Rynders federal marshal of New York, a plum piece of patronage, an office in which the captain could enrich himself in a dozen different ways.

Isaiah Rynders was at the height of his power when he met Albert Hicks. The first shots of the Civil War, which would upend everything—the entire era would be sealed in amber, relegated to the antebellum past—were just a few months away. Rynders did not personally involve himself in every murder case, but this one was special. What had happened on the *E. A. Johnson* was not just a killing, not just three killings, not just a slaughter—it was a sensation. It touched the deepest fears and obsessions of the city, toyed with its subconscious. Hicks was the nightmare that stalked your dreams. Rynders wanted to meet him because he was curious but also because there was money to be made.

Rynders at first was interested in simply looking the killer over, getting a sense of him, making sure, in the way of a riverboat gambler, that this was indeed the man. He talked to Hicks, looked in his eyes, tried to tease out his cascade of monosyllabic answers. No, no, no—that was all Hicks said.

First order of business for Rynders? Clear the crowd that lingered in front of the police station. Hundreds were standing on the steps, disrupting traffic. Rynders did it in the way of the sharpie, a two-part operation meant to satisfy and confuse the mob.

One: Hicks was "conducted into the main office of the Marshal, where he remained for an hour and a half, during which time scores of persons were permitted to enter and gratify their curiosity by looking at the criminal," according to Elias Smith. Hicks meanwhile "sat handcuffed in one corner of the room, and met the scrutinizing gaze of his multitude of visitors without betraying the slightest emotion of any kind. In fact he did not appear from his actions to be conscious that he was any more the object of curiosity than anyone else in the crowd. He is not vicious-looking, and the universal expression of those who see him, for the first time, is that of disappointment in finding so 'good-looking a man,' when they expected to behold a monster."

Two: "While the prisoner was thus undergoing the inspection of those who were so fortunate as to gain admission to the Marshal's office, the large and increasing throng outside were made the victims of an ingenious maneuver, which exhibited the tact of Capt. Rynders in dissipating a crowd," Smith went on. "A man named Curtis, recently convicted of forgery, and about to be conveyed to Sing Sing, was taken through the Marshal's office, handcuffed and in charge of officers, and let out by a pri-

vate door opening in Chambers Street. The crowd, supposing the man to be Hicks, ran off en masse in pursuit of
the officers, shouting 'There he is—that's him—that's
him.' The dodge created much merriment among those
inside the Marshal's office, and none laughed heartier or
seemed to enjoy the joke more than the prisoner."

The process of building a case against Hicks got under
way at once. Rynders began by bringing in witnesses to
identify the fugitive. *Is this the person you saw on the
ship, yawl, ferry, street, etc.?* A modern lineup consists of
a handful of people of various makes, sizes, and ages
standing beside a suspect. If the witness picks the suspected killer out of the line, the identification is considered made. Rynders used an older method, more like a
3D lineup or diorama. He filled a room in the precinct
house with gangsters and sailors, many of them his own
soldiers from the Sixth Ward, then brought witnesses in
one at a time. The marshal told them to wander through
the room as they would wander through a saloon until
they found the man they'd seen on the ship, yawl, ferry,
street, etc.

Abram Egbert, who had talked to Hicks at Vanderbilt's ferry landing on Staten Island; Augustus Gisler, who
had served the pirate oysters and eggs in Peter Van Pelt's
saloon; Selah Howell, the co-owner of the *E. A. Johnson*
who had had dinner with Hicks on the sloop; Burke, the
superintendent of the Cedar Street tenement—each man
wandered the room till he found Hicks. William Drumm,
who had carried the big seabag through the city, stood
five feet from the suspect, pointing and shouting, "That's
him—that's the man! I asked for fifty cents. He gave me
three shillings."

Policemen and gangsters stood around smiling and laughing. They doted on their chief, Isaiah Rynders, who sat on the edge of a desk, pipe in hand, talking. "About two dozen persons were in the room," according to a reporter on the scene, "the most conspicuous of whom was the redoubtable Captain Rynders, who passed the time telling anecdotes, and amongst other things stated that five murderers were now in his custody, and if they caught John Chinaman that would make six." (John Chinaman went otherwise unidentified, another untold New York story.) Hicks "took his hat off and appeared as if he [suddenly] realized the position he was in," the reporter went on. "His head and features indicate him to be a man of brutal propensities—one who could knock another one down on the slightest provocation, being a large, strong, and powerful-looking man."

The police brought in the prisoner's wife. They wanted to find out how much she knew—could she be charged as an accomplice? Elias Smith saw her in the station waiting for the marshal, holding her eleven-month-old son. She seemed bewildered. She wept, stopped weeping, then wept again. Myopia gave her gaze a lost, unfocused quality.

The investigators spoke to her alone. At first, she could not believe her husband had done these things. She had never known him to be anything other than honest. When she'd asked him about the windfall, he'd told her it came from the salvage of an abandoned ship. Why wouldn't she believe him? He was her husband. The police came to trust and even pity her. She had, in a sense, been a victim along with the others.

She said she'd been terrified when she first read about

the *E. A. Johnson* in the newspaper and had warned her husband, *You must be careful; there's a killer on the sea.* She'd actually read him the article. This is likely when Hicks learned that the ship had not been scuttled, but was in fact in the possession of the police.

"How'd he respond?" asked a detective.

"He listened for a time," said Mrs. Hicks, then told her he was sleepy and didn't want to hear any more.

The police brought Mrs. Hicks to see her husband in his cell. It was their first meeting since the arrest. It had only been thirty hours, but it might as well have been a century. She stood at the bars, cursing. She called him a scoundrel, the worst kind of villain. He swore he was innocent and demanded she believe him. It went back and forth. Finally she held the baby up and shouted, "Look at your offspring, you rascal, and think what you have brought on us. If I could get at you, I would pull your bloody heart out."

"[Hicks] looked at her coolly," according to a report, "and quietly replied, 'Why, my dear wife, I've done nothing—it will be all out in a day or two.'"

On her way to the street, Mrs. Hicks fell into the arms of Elias Smith, the reporter. "What can I do?" she cried. "I can't go to my parents at Albany; I would not carry my disgrace home to them."

THE TRIAL

She was never given a first name, in court records, city files, or newspaper stories. She was only Mrs. Hicks, the prisoner's wife, a weak-eyed woman, the sore-eyed missus, betrothed to a killer. Maybe this was done as a courtesy, to keep the names of the innocent out of the whirlwind. Maybe it was done because she was seen as no more than an appendage, a woman in a man's world of lawyers, detectives, sailors, and pirates. She remains a mystery as a result, a stand-in for all those on the periphery, out of the spotlight but still on the stage. What was she like? What did she really believe? What happened to her?

Mrs. Hicks's story is there, though, between the lines, in the asides in the court transcripts, in the background information written by reporters and cops. A small, near-sighted Irish immigrant, she'd been in America less than ten years at the time of her husband's arrest. She had met

Hicks on the *Isaac Wright,* the ship that brought her family from Ireland to America in 1853. She had been traveling with her mother, father, brother, and sisters, escaping Ireland's hardship and famine. She probably spotted Hicks, who was working on the ship as a carpenter, on deck amid other workingmen. Perhaps he noticed her right away. Perhaps she noticed him noticing her. At some point, he introduced himself. Their exchanges grew long and personal. Perhaps they stood together in the wind and rain. It took at least ten days to sail from Dublin to New York, and in that time, you were almost certain to get the kind of weather that would cause even normally reserved strangers to cling together.

One day Hicks turned up beside her family. He'd brought them bread. More visits and more treats followed. He was reaching out a hand; she took it. She was a poor emigrant on her way to an unknown, unimaginable country. He was an American, handsome, and secure. He was with her when she first saw Manhattan. Viewed from the east, the city seems to rise from the sea, first the far-off tower of Trinity Church, announcing the island with an exclamation, then the wharves and the pier sheds, warehouses and limestone buildings, the green Battery, the brick houses beyond Peck Slip, the great avenues.

Once her family found lodgings in the city, Hicks visited the apartment where they stayed. Her parents did not approve. There was something unsettling about him. It was there in his eyes. The family moved upstate, a not uncommon choice for immigrants looking to escape the degradation of the Fourth Ward or the Five Points. For less than a dollar, you could ride a ferry from Manhattan to Albany, a beautiful steamer that filled the night sky with sparks. Above Washington Heights, the river is punctuated by islands and bays, blue mist shrouds the hills that recede into wilderness. Is this what America looked like to Thomas Jefferson? They'd pass West Point, lofty on its palisade, Cold Spring, Beacon, Rhinebeck, Catskill, and Hudson, bustling towns where you could stumble into the rest of your life.

They settled on the edge of Albany, a city booming on the river trade. Hicks visited every few months, bringing presents—amethyst, mother-of-pearl, gems from beyond the sea. Sometimes he was flush; other times he was broke. Sometimes he was moody; other times ebullient. They went for rides in the country, or sat in the shade of the hemlock trees. Her parents urged her to break it off. *Where does this man come from? Where does he go? How does he come to have so much money? How does he lose it? Where is his family?* Two cards in the tarot deck were visible, but the rest had been dealt facedown.

She'd been warned, but she was twenty-three and getting older every minute. They were married in April 1853. They settled first in Norwich, Connecticut, where Hicks worked in a shop until he tired of it. That was how he was—restless, continually overcome by a need for variety. Boredom was a driving force in his life. He could do something only so long, then gave it up. He was constantly short of money as a result. It troubled the marriage. She went to her family for loans again and again. At first, they gave what they could. Then they refused. She and Hicks moved to New York City, where he set her up in a tiny apartment, two rooms on Batavia Street, in lower Manhattan—then went to sea. He hauled sugar, then cotton. Back in Connecticut, he worked for a doctor named Baldwin until he got restless. Again to New York, 129 Cedar Street. When he returned from sea that last time, it was with more cash than she'd ever seen. She believed they were about to start a new life, a real life. They had become parents. He was a good father and loved the boy.

When the detectives arrested Hicks, the floor beneath her fell away. Nothing lay below but ruin and despair. The day after the arrest, she had followed her husband to New York, crying as she held the child. When she learned the true nature of his crimes . . . it was more than a person could fathom, everything her parents had warned her about times a million. Those facedown tarot cards turned out to include the Devil and the Hanged Man.

For a few weeks she stayed away from Hicks, then began visiting him in jail. It might be hard to believe that she returned to this homicidal husband, resumed their relationship, and even came to love him again, but who else did she have? He was the father of her child, her only friend. As sleep is more important than sex, companionship is more important than disgust. Did she forgive Hicks? Would she remember him when he was gone, or wipe it all away and start clean? Did she tell her son who his father had been? All that is lost, unknowable, at the bottom of the river.

The police worried about her. Small, weak-eyed, and alone, she carried the weight of the world. And the child! And those sad rooms on Cedar Street! What would become of her? Hart Weed, who ran the second precinct, wrote the federal government and asked that she be given money. *Please help this pitiful woman.*

Isolated, running out of money, she finally wrote her

mother in Albany. According to Robert Frost, "Home is the place where, when you have to go there, they have to take you in." Her mother wrote back, a letter that survives. The syntax and many of the details are confusing, with inside references and allusions—the family was apparently named Bunting; a sister had seemingly married a man named Salters—but the general washing-of-the-hands sentiment will be familiar to anyone who's ever been abandoned in a crisis.

> *Albany, April 18, 1860.*
> *. . . I understand that your husband is charged of a very serious crime, and, as you want me to direct you how to act, I cannot advise you, under such circumstances, how to act. You have always been wanting something since you got married to him. You wanting at one time over one hundred dollars, and you would take all the Salters has and would do no good. I have got nothing for you, nor for myself, and have to depend on a strange man for my own support, as none of my children would support me; and as you want to be advised, I cannot say what is best for you to do, unless you adopt your child and live out. I cannot do nothing for you, and as for your sister and Salters, they do not want to hear any more from you and Johnson, for he got tired helping you and him, and done no good, and as besides Salters does not want you to come near him. He thinks a great disgrace of such a thing; he has a very large family to support, and you cannot expect anything from him. You would not take his advice, he told you not to marry John-*

*son, as you knew nothing about him; so as you
made your bed, you must lie. You are young, and
go to work; you will be better without Johnson,
anyways; and if you think you cannot work, there
is a place, for you can go to the Shakers, and have
a good home there. But I think there is no chance
for him to escape, so I have no more to say, but
remain your mother till death,*
Rebecca Bunting

Albert Hicks was moved to the big prison on Centre
Street, officially named the Halls of Justice, but no one
called it that. Around this time the explorer and diplomat
John L. Stephens toured the Middle East, then published
a book that included drawings of wonders he had seen
there. Someone noticed that Manhattan's new lockup
looked a lot like the Egyptian mausoleum in Stephens's
book and gave the jail its unofficial name: the Tombs.
About twenty years old when Hicks arrived, the Tombs
was considered an improvement over the primitive jails it
replaced. Consisting of two massive buildings, it covered
the block bound by Centre, Elm (now Lafayette), Franklin, and Leonard streets. It was built on the shoddy fill
that erased the city's bucolic pond, the Collect. Some said
the Tombs was actually built on the island that sat at the
center of that pond, the site of the city's first gallows,
where dozens of men, including the leaders of New York's
slave insurrection of 1741, were executed.

The Tombs was three prisons under a single roof: one
for men, one for women, and one for boys. Above a
courtyard, a skyway carried prisoners from the admitting

office to the cells. It was dubbed the Bridge of Sighs, after a Venetian walkway that led from that city's palace to that city's jail: as prisoners crossed it, legend goes, they'd look back at Venice and sigh. The top floors of the Tombs were for petty criminals—pickpockets, brawlers, drunks. Bank robbers and bunco artists were kept on tiers two and three. The worst prisoners lived on the ground floor, where the swamp stink of the Collect lingered in the drains. The jail was built for two hundred inmates but housed twice as many when Hicks lived there. Even then it was considered the sort of cruel place where the trial becomes the punishment. Charles Dickens, who visited the Tombs on one of his trips to America, called it a "dismal-fronted pile of bastard Egyptian, like an enchanter's palace in a melodrama! Why, such indecent and disgusting as these cells, would bring disgrace upon the most despotic empire in the world!"

Hicks was kept in the strip of cells occupied by the prison's most dangerous men, the so-called Murderers' Corridor. Cell 8. There was corruption even here. Wealthy inmates were allowed to bring in their own finery and food. One prisoner, Richard Robinson, had meals catered by Delmonico's, the great New York restaurant. His cell was decked out in Louis XIV furniture: a velvet couch, a canopy bed. A drawing of him eating an oyster-topped filet in his cell was widely circulated. Charles Sutton, a longtime warden of the prison, described such a scene in his 1874 book *The New York Tombs:* "In a patent extension chair [the rich prisoner] lolls, smoking an aromatic Havana, while he reads the proceedings of his trial the day previous in the morning papers. He has an elegant dressing gown on, faced with cherry colored silk, and his feet are encased in delicately worked slippers. . . . His lunch [is] not cooked in the prison but brought in from a hotel. It consists of a variety of dishes, such as quail on toast, game pates, reed birds, ortolans, fowl, the newest vegetables, coffee, cognac."

Hicks had no money, thus no special meals, no soft mattress. Just the basic setup: damp cell, iron bars. And yet in those first weeks, his mood seemed placid, even fine. He was so adamant about his innocence and so certain of his exoneration that he convinced many of those around him. You can see it in a story published in one of the downtown papers a few days after he arrived in the Tombs. The reporter spoke to the convict through the bars.

At 3 1/2 o'clock our reporter paid HICKS a visit, and found him in the murderer's corridor, ground floor, occupying cell No. 8. He had just been furnished with a new straw bed, on which he sat smoking a cheap cigar, and contemplating with apparent indifference his novel and comfortable abode. The following dialogue occurred:

Reporter—Well, my friend, how do you like your new quarters? [Your digs] look rather comfortable, eh?

Prisoner—Well, yes; they do very well. [Pause.] Are you one of the keepers?

R.—No, I am a reporter.

P.—A what?

R.—A reporter; if you have anything to say that you would like published, I will take it down—nothing like hearing both sides. [Long pause.] I believe you have stated that you were not on board the sloop E.A. Johnson. Is that so?

P.—Yes. I never saw the sloop. I never knew Capt. BURR, nor heard of him. I never was on an oyster boat in my life; the last boat I was on was the Geo. Darly. Now you put that down, will you?

R.—All right—down it goes; what else? Where did the Darly sail from?

P.—She sailed from Peck-slip.

R.—Where to?

P.—To Charleston.

R.—How long ago was that?

P.—[After a long pause]—Well, I should think it was a month and a half since I got back here. I was gone three weeks.

R.—Where have you been since?

P.—Well, when I got back from Charleston I went to Fall River by steamboat. In a few days I came back to New-York and stayed here three days—then went back to Fall River again, and have not been in New-York since, until last Wednesday morning. I arrived here in the Fall River boat, and returned on the same boat in the evening.

R.—You will be able to show then that you were in Fall River all this time?

P.—Yes, my counsel has gone on to see about it now.

. . .

R.—Well, how about that watch? How did you get Capt. BURR's watch if you never knew him? I suppose you are aware that it has been identified by the jeweler who cleaned it?

P.—Well, he will have to prove he cleaned it, won't he?

R.—He has got the record of it, with the number of the watch, and Capt. BURR's name.

P.—Well, I don't know anything about that; it's my watch.

R.—Did you see Mr. HOWELL up at the Marshal's office to-day?

P.—Who?

R.—Mr. HOWELL, of Islip, Long Island; he was up there and identified you as the man that took supper with him and Capt. BURR on board the sloop E.A. Johnson, the night before she sailed. He says you sat on his left and Capt. BURR on his right.

P.—Oh, he's mistaken; it was some other man; he never saw me in his life.

HICKS here stepped back into his cell, and commenced shaking up his new bed.

R.—You'll be all right; if you can prove you have been in Fall River all this time, you'll get out of it.

P.—Indeed I shall; yes, Sir, I'll get out of it all right.

HICKS here stepped back into his cell, and commenced shaking up his new bed.

This would strike a careful reader as a tell, not a confession perhaps, but an expression of stress, a guilty man retreating when presented with evidence of his crime. Note how, when the reporter attempted to buck up the prisoner—"You'll be all right"—he did not express innocence but merely his certainty that he will "get out of it all right."

Hicks had retained the services of two defense attorneys. Freemasons like the prisoner, they probably considered the work an obligation of brotherhood. And a hedge—in the next world, the jailed man might be a prince or lord. When asked to describe his counsel, Hicks would merely hand over a business card: Graves & Sayles, Attorneys.

Sayles was a hustling young lawyer, a court rat constantly on the lookout for the case that would make his name. In Hicks, he would have seen not only a Masonic brother in a jam but also a ticket to the big time. You represent a notorious man, you'll be all over the press. And his partner Graves? Well, every wizard needs someone to fill that second seat.

Sayles and Graves started by sitting down with their client and hearing him out. *Why don't you tell us what happened?* Hicks said there was not much to tell as he knew nothing more of the killings than what had been read to him from the newspaper. He said he had not even been in New York at the time of the killings. "I haven't been here, before now, for at least two or three months." Which made things easy. Forget the compass and the watch and the other physical evidence—the defense lawyers need only to establish an alibi, a hotel registry or a person who could place Hicks out of town at the time of the killings. Maybe the killers *had* been river pirates, or some other variety of thug, but none of that really mattered. All they had to do was show that Hicks had not been in New York, and the prosecutor's case would fall apart.

In search of an alibi, the attorneys went to Fall River, a booming port on the Taunton River—you go through Fall River on the way to Cape Cod—tuned to the rhythm of the Atlantic tide. This was, after all, a story of the sea, of sailors and sloops, the great watery world. The attorneys spent two days knocking on doors and looking at documents, questioning friends and old neighbors. They found many people who had known Hicks or the family— there were several Hicks siblings—but none who had seen Albert recently or could place him in Fall River on the day in question. Asking leading questions did not help, nor did dropping hints or making suggestions. They could not even find anyone willing to lie or misremember for their client.

They returned to Manhattan dejected, but Hicks did not seem concerned. What did he think would happen? Did he think a solution would emerge from the ether? Did he think a trail of light would appear in the Tombs, and he would follow it through an open door? His brother Simon had been in a similar fix—jailed in Connecticut for murder, scheduled to hang—but he had slipped away, as if by a miracle, in a jailbreak, never to be seen again. *Sonofabitch is probably belly up to a frontier bar right this minute!* Did the luck of Simon Hicks give Albert Hicks a false sense of possibility, faith that a gate would open and he too would slip away? Simon was out there, just above the prison wall, highballing it across the evening sky.

Albert Hicks told his counsel to write to his older brother, Arnold. He was the best of them, educated and rich, with a house in East Killingly, Connecticut. He'd always looked after the younger members of the family. If Arnold were brought to understand the gravity of the situation, he would surely remember something. The attorneys wrote, signed, and sent the letter.

The response came a few weeks later:

EAST KILLINGLY, Thursday, April 26, 1860
GENTLEMEN: I received your letter of the 24th,
in regard to my brother's present circumstances
and future prospects; and in reply would say that
no one can feel more keenly in regard to his condi-
tion than I do—but justice must, in my case at
least, triumph over brotherly love. The chain of
circumstances against him is conclusive proof, yea,
more than that, that he is guilty of the crimes prof-
fered against him. You speak of his case as looking
more favorable than it did; but I do not under-
stand that anything has come to light to make an
impression on the public mind that he is innocent.
The only way for him to evade the arm of justice is
in regard to the point of jurisdiction, and every one
must be aware, if that point can be settled so as to
bring him to trial, there is no escape. Believe me,
gentlemen, if I had a princely fortune, and believed,
or had the least reason to believe, that my brother
was innocent, I would willingly sacrifice it all in
his behalf; but when a man so far forgets his duty
to God and man as to stain his hands with human
blood, though he were my own brother, I would
sign his death-warrant.

You may think these are unnatural feelings for
one brother to have toward another, but in reply, I
would say, unnatural deeds produce unnatural
feelings; and though it pains me to the very heart
when I reflect on his condition, yet when, in my
imagination, I see the ghosts of Capt. BURR and
the two WATTS boys arise from their watery beds,
and point to him as the unmistakable cause—and

when I contemplate the anguish and suffering of the friends of these murdered men, all my finer feelings vanish, and I sincerely hope that he will never escape through the weakness of the law.

In regard to our circumstances you have been misinformed. There is not one of his brothers that is in a situation to help defend him, even if he were innocent. As to his wife and child, though strangers to us, they have our warmest sympathies in this trying affair, and I would afford them substantial aid if I were in circumstances to admit of it. For proof of our circumstances, and that myself and brothers are not such as you have been led to believe, I refer you to ALMOND M. PAINE, Judge of Probate, and Dr. E. A. HILL, Postmaster at East Killingly, Conn.

After having thus written my honest feelings in regard to my unnatural brother's affairs, allow me to subscribe myself,
Gentlemen,

Your obedient servant,
Signed,
ARNOLD HICKS

Meanwhile Albert Hicks had become an antihero in New York. On the eve of the Civil War, the city was as economically stratified as it is today. The wealthiest New Yorkers, the aristocrats and tycoons, had fled lower Manhattan, leaving the old blocks to the indigent immigrant Irish, and headed uptown to Fourth and Fifth avenues,

where, in brownstone mansions and town houses, protected by an ever more modern police force, they created
an enclave. It was a different world above Fourteenth
Street. Downtown, the poorest had taken over areas
abandoned by the rich, waterfront wards where wooden
mansions dilapidated into rooming houses and elegant
streets turned into slums. The middle class, small but
growing, was squeezed between. Clerks and merchants,
salesmen, physicians, and journalists lived in apartments
and houses on Ninth and Tenth streets, on Fourth Avenue
and Broadway, in the Fifteenth and Eighteenth Wards in
Gramercy Park and Union Square. They dreamed of as-
cension, the grand move to the upper city, but they feared
decline—a slump back into the swamp.

This world, where the climb never ended and there
was no limit to the rich and their airs, turned Hicks from
psychotic killer to idol. A son of a bitch, yes, but our son
of a bitch, a man who defied the traditional authority of
cops and millionaires. Its denizens came to invent, then
believe the story that Hicks had been shanghaied. If he
had not been shanghaied, then he was a monster. But if
he'd been kidnapped from a Cherry Street crimp, drugged
and stolen away, he could be seen as almost righteous.
Put in a situation that seemed to dramatize the situation
of so many—forced into the dregs, ordered to work or
swim—he had struck back. The shanghai story did not
stand up to scrutiny, but who was scrutinizing it? As a
result, and again like today, you had two stories: the one
being told in the *Times,* and the one being told on the
streets. Those who knew nothing else about Albert Hicks
knew that he terrified the shipowners and moneylenders
and police. For many, that was enough.

Within a week of his arrest, Hicks was a star. It was the brutality of the murders, the hurried escape, the flight from the cops. It was the whiskey, the oysters and eggs. It was how good he looked in shackles. It was the way he smiled, then turned away. It was his steely calm, scratchy beard, pearl-white teeth, and black eyes. It was his chilling laugh. He had quickly become a household name, analyzed and discussed by the most powerful people in New York. It was the mesmerizing aura of the killer, which is irresistible if that killer is a knockout. A powerful charisma settles around anyone mad enough to live outside the law. Our history of great leaders is paralleled by a history of great psychotics—Jean Lafitte, Al Capone, Louis Lepke. Something about these men remains mysterious, unknowable, and it fascinates. Their lives suggest a different kind of existence, lives without God, lives that are truly and terribly free.

People began showing up at the Tombs, hoping to catch a glimpse of Hicks. If they could just see him, get close, ask a question . . . Important visitors were allowed in and stood staring through the bars. A common person might slip a coin into the hand of a guard and be taken, late in the day, for a walk along Murderers' Corridor. Hicks said all the attention made him feel "like a monkey in a cage."

Some showed up in groups, after drinks, slumming. Others came with a confidant or two. A particularly noteworthy visitor arrived by himself shortly before Hicks was to make his first appearance in court. He asked the warden, Charles Sutton, if he could meet with the infamous prisoner. Pressed on the nature of his business, the tall, stout man handed over his card: P. T. Barnum,

Showman. When told of it, Hicks laughed and said, "Oh, Barnum's on the make. If he's of a kind to pay, let him come and I'll make my own bargain."

The warden led Barnum through a maze of cells to Murderers' Corridor. Barnum, a doughy man nearing fifty, favored three-piece suits, hooked a fat thumb in his watch pocket, and grinned. Half his head was bald, the other half awash in curly dark hair. He'd been born in Bethel, Connecticut, at the start of the nineteenth century. A product of the old star-lit agrarian world, he'd help create our modern sensibility, which is nothing but spectacle and hokum. He started out as a straight-down-the-middle merchant, but his cynical sense of human nature and wicked sense of moneymaking fun was too developed to be confined to the provinces. He moved to Manhattan in 1835, going first into the theater, then into a more general ballyhoo. He began by producing sidewalk freak shows with bearded ladies and rubber men. At Niblo's Garden, he caused a stir by selling tickets to see Joice Heth, an old black woman whom Barnum claimed had been a wet-nurse to George Washington, which would have made her 161 years old.

In 1850 Barnum brought the opera singer Jenny Lind, "the Swedish Nightingale," whom he dubbed "the most famous person in Europe," to New York to perform at Castle Garden, an auditorium that stood on a North River island where cars currently enter the Brooklyn-Battery Tunnel. Lind did ninety-three shows. By the end of the run, Barnum was himself a superstar. He'd already opened his American Museum, on the corner of Ann Street and Broadway, in a racy neighborhood of taverns and gambling joints, the sort known as wolf traps, deadfalls, or ten percent houses. Across the street stood the most famous of these, Tap Franc, featuring the first roulette wheel in New York, as well as regular tables for faro, blackjack, and a three-dice game called Chuck-a-Luck.

Barnum's museum was popular with the sort of people New York critics dismissed as yokels or country cousins; that is, the same sort who turned Albert Hicks into an antihero. This mob was fixated by outlandish tales in the penny press. Barnum knew the path to their wallets in the instinctive way of an artist; hence his museum's never-ending stream of astonishing exhibits: the four-legged chicken and the two-headed calf, the armless wonder, the wild men of Borneo, the Fiji mermaid—a monkey torso attached to the body of a fish—the snake charmer, the albino, the glass eater and the mental marvel, the ossified girl, the man who never smiles, wax replicas of notorious outlaws and western heroes. Barnum staged the wedding of midget Tom Thumb to midget Lavinia Warren in Grace Church. It was covered by the *Times*—neither on the wedding nor the society page but as a spectacle so out-landish it constituted news.

Barnum's first museum stood for just twenty-four years, from 1841 to 1865 (it burned down, was rebuilt, then burned again), yet it was one of the incubators of modern culture. It was Barnum who created the Times Square energy, the spectacle and the con that, other than the Bill of Rights, is about all we have left of old America. The movies and vast entertainment zones, Disney World

and Las Vegas, Spider-Man, rock 'n' roll, our current politics—it all grew out of P. T. Barnum's original insight: believing is seeing.

Barnum stood outside the prison bars, smiling at Hicks. He introduced himself, then got down to business. He wanted to make a plaster mold of Hicks's face and use it to re-create the killer in wax. "I will display the figure prominently in my museum. It will be seen by millions!"

"Why would you want to do that?"

"Because you are famous. People stand in the street even now, in the rain, hoping to see you but not all can be satisfied," said Barnum. "We will give them that satisfaction."

Hicks had no use for money, never would again. But his thoughts turned to his wife and child. If he could make a little cash for them, then maybe get an extra something for himself . . . Terms were quickly reached. For twenty-five dollars cash and two boxes of five-cent cigars, Hicks would allow Barnum to cast his face in plaster.

The trial was held in a new building at 39 Chambers between Centre Street and Broadway, across from City Hall. This was New York as imagined by its first fathers—marble columns, with grand stone steps leading up from the street. The U.S. Circuit Court was on the second floor, Judge Smalley presiding. He was known to be a clear-eyed commonsensical judge, fast but fair. He knew all men of note in the legal community—it was still a small city. Just a few restaurants, taverns, clubs. Everything was personal; everyone was conflicted.

Albert Hicks would be prosecuted by a team of lawyers handpicked by U.S. District Attorney James I. Roosevelt, who'd previously served as a member of the U.S. Congress and as a New York State Supreme Court justice. Roosevelt, the grandfather of the future president Teddy Roosevelt, is referred to in accounts as ex-Judge Roosevelt. He selected attorney James Dwight to try the case. Dwight bursts from court transcripts like a lawyer in a Movie of the Week, smart and moralistic, partial to dramatic turns of phrase and the sort of courtroom comedy that catches you by surprise. The case must have been important to Dwight—only a few times in life, if ever, will you get a chance to impress your sensibility on your city.

It was Dwight who explained why the government was charging Hicks with piracy instead of murder. To prove murder you needed a body or, in this case, three bodies. Though the police were still combing the beaches, the accused had apparently made sure no bodies would ever be found. The best they could do with a standard charge was robbery, which would mean—what?—ten years in Sing Sing? Twenty? For a triple murder? Intolerable. Piracy, though based on a somewhat obscure federal statute passed by Congress in 1820, was an infinitely better charge.

Dwight read the statute to the court: "If any person shall upon the high seas, or in any open roadstead, or in any haven, basin or bay, or in any river where the sea ebbs and flows, commit any robbery in, or upon any ship or vessel, or the lading thereof, such person shall be adjudged to be a pirate; and being thereof convicted before the Circuit Court of the United States for the District into which he shall be brought, or in which he shall be found, shall suffer death."

In other words, if you rob on the water, you are a pirate. If you are a pirate, you shall suffer the traditional pirate punishment—hanging by the neck till dead.

Defense Attorney Sayles argued against the applicability of this law. Piracy meant the open sea, Sayles told the judge, beyond Sandy Hook, where the coastal shelf falls away and the water goes from sky blue to black. But the *E. A. Johnson* was found in the Lower Bay, a mile from Staten Island, well within the jurisdiction of Harbor Patrol, that is, New York City. This entire case, explained Sayles, was as local as Delmonico's or Trinity Church. Piracy? Just how far could you stretch a statute to reach a desired result? If the government wanted to put his client to death, it had to prove murder.

Judge Smalley considered this argument, which, on its face, seemed reasonable, then rejected it. He was fixed on the larger duty of the court, which was to uphold societal stability and bring justice. He understood legalism but followed common sense. Just look at the defendant, with the sneer and the stubble, the rope-scarred hands and crow-black eyes. What did he look like? A pirate. So that was how he would be tried.

The defense then asked that the trial be moved to a different jurisdiction, far from the coast. In a case that had become a public obsession, flooding the newspapers with rumor and falsehood, how could enough unbiased men possibly be found to form a jury?

Smalley rejected this argument, too. The idea of an untainted jury, a perfect group of wise but unknowing men, was fantasy, he explained. Maybe it existed in the next world, but in this world, with its dirty port and its rough sea, there was no such thing as a perfect arbiter.

That was why we had twelve, that was why we called for belief beyond a reasonable doubt. That was why the verdict had to be unanimous.

"Judge SMALLEY, we are glad to see, has pronounced against the attempt to introduce into the Federal Courts, in the Hicks case, the absurd rule, so stringently enforced in our State Courts, that the mere fact of a man's having read the comments or reports of a newspaper, on the commission of a crime, shall disqualify him for acting as a juryman on the trial," the *Times* editorialized on May 16, 1860.

> That such a doctrine should have ever secured recognition in the United States, the country of newspapers par excellence, is, perhaps, one of the oddest and most unaccountable of the oddities of Anglo-Saxon law. It would be natural and reasonable enough if promulgated in Austria or Russia, where newspapers rank as unavoidable nuisances, the general use of which it is one of the first duties of the Government to discourage. But in America every man reads the newspapers who knows how to read at all, or who is fit to take part in any judicial proceeding. When a great crime is committed which causes a general sensation, everybody reads the report of it—if he knows how to read; and if he does not know how, he is not fit to sit on a jury. So that the question with which every man on the panel is assailed in the State Courts, on a criminal trial, by the prisoner's counsel, as to whether he has read the newspaper reports touching the prisoner and his offence, is in reality equivalent to ask-

ing him: "Are you so stupid and ignorant that,
living in New-York, you cannot read or understand a daily paper? Or if you read one, are you
such a piece of eccentricity, as without any motive
in the world, carefully to avoid perusing any allu-
sion it contains to a subject of which every man
and woman around you is talking?"

Jury selection took two days. The names of the jurors
reflect the city as it was before the great immigrant flood
filled its directories with Russian, Polish, Slavic, Chinese,
Indian, and Spanish names. The fact that no women
served—they would not get the vote for another sixty
years—goes without saying. This was a study in Anglo-
Saxon (English and Scottish), white males:

Bernard McElroy
Owen Foley
John Coulter
Geo. W. Jackson
Jas. C. Rhodes
Isaac Jerome
Andrew Brady
Robert W. Allen
John Farrell
James N. Fuller
John McCalvey
Benjamin Sherman

The trial began on Monday, May 14, 1860. People
stood in the street hoping to catch a glimpse of Hicks as
he was led up the courthouse steps between Marshal

Rynders and a deputy. The prisoner wore heavy irons to court but did not seem especially troubled or weighted down. He was, according to the *New York Post*, "respectably dressed in black cloth pantaloons, dark colored vest and black cloth sack coat. A heavy blue scarf was around his neck, hiding his collar. His long black hair was neatly brushed back, and his general appearance evidenced considerable attention to his toilette. In conversation Johnson [aka Hicks] is rather pleasing than otherwise, evincing both intelligence and shrewdness. His manner is much more refined than the published reports would lead one to suppose."

Judge Smalley arrived at 11:15 A.M. The irons had been removed from Hicks, who stood when the judge entered.

Asked to state his name, the prisoner spoke softly: "My name is William Johnson. My right name is Albert W. Hicks."

"Have you anything to say in regard to this charge?"

"No, sir."

"The prisoner then sat down," according to the *Post*. "He appeared flushed, and his brows were closely knitted."

The prosecutor addressed the jury. He promised not to bore them with a traditional opening statement. The details of this case had been so carefully chronicled, he explained, and the facts were so well known, that it would be patronizing to pretend that you knew nothing. *We all understand what this man is charged with and what sort of outrage we believe he has committed. This is your city. We simply ask that you do what must be done.*

Dwight summarized the facts nevertheless, in broad outline: the discovery of the *E. A. Johnson,* the state of its cabin and decks, the missing money, the vanished men. "The bowsprit of the vessel was broken off, and its rigging trailing in the water," the prosecutor said. "The sails were down, and the boom of the vessel, which had been set, was over the side of the vessel. There was no human being found on the vessel, and no light. Forward of the mast appeared a large pool of blood which had run down to some cordage and sticks at the back of the mast, and also down the side of the vessel into the sea. This was just aft the forecastle hatch, on which, or near which, was found some hair—a lock of hair."

The prosecutor listed the stolen items: $150 in gold and silver coins, $26 in paper currency, a daguerreotype of a young woman, a pair of pantaloons, a felt hat, a gold ring, a silver watch that belonged to Captain Burr, a sea compass. He named the victims, lingered on details of their shortened lives, what they would never do, the ripple effect of their deaths on those who loved them. He explained the particulars of the charge, why it was not necessary to prove Hicks had done the killing to reach a guilty verdict on piracy. "Each little item of evidence is of no particular strength," he went on, "of no decision in itself, but only [matters in part of] forming a strong chain, a perfect chain, that, as claimed by the government, fixing without question and without doubt the guilt of this offence [piracy] on the prisoner."

The courtroom was filled with family members of the victims, except for Captain Burr's wife, who'd suffered a mental breakdown and been hospitalized. There were reporters too, dozens of them, and curiosity seekers. They listened to the prosecutor but watched the accused, who sat calmly at the defense table, his hands folded before him, head down. The newspapers paid close attention to his demeanor, describing it as reserved, detached. Onlookers wanted to know how the bad man was taking it—would he give in, crack, confess? They wanted him to break but also to stay in character. Once a man put on that mask, he should keep it on till he dies.

Dwight ended not with the murders or the thefts but with luck—the great good luck that the police had in catching this man, who should have been home free the moment he reached Staten Island. The prosecutor asked the jury to consider where such luck might come from and what it might mean. "It seems strange in this center of swarming thousands, at such a time of day as the prisoner escaped from that sloop, he could not have hidden himself. It seems as though there was but one eye to watch, and one instinct to follow and observe him."

But whose eye was that?

Hicks thought he had sunk the ship and buried the bodies in five fathoms of water, but the eye had been watching. Hicks thought he'd changed the money and gotten away, but there was the eye. Was it the eye of Hart Weed, the police captain? Or of George Nevins, the detective? No, said the prosecutor, these men were merely mechanisms. The eye stood above and beyond all, unblinking as the killer fled across the country. The eye had brought the chase to Albert Hicks and seen that he was carried back here, where it watched still, to see that the jury ended the story with justice.

What could the defense attorney say after that?

Sayles spoke of jurisdiction (the robbery did not occur

on the high seas but in New York Harbor) and coincidence (the prosecutor's entire case was circumstantial), then sat and waited for the trial to begin.

Selah Howell was the first witness called on the first day. He'd been co-owner of the *E. A. Johnson,* a businessman and shipbuilder; he'd designed the sloop. He said he'd visited Captain Burr at the Spring Street pier the night before it sailed. He talked to the captain on deck, then had dinner with the captain and his first mate, Hicks. Burr sat on one side, Hicks on the other. Hicks did not say much, but no doubt, said Howell, he was the man now at the defense table.

Hicks glared. Howell held the glare as he described the current condition of the ship. The *E. A. Johnson* had been returned to him after spending six days at the Fulton Fish Market pier. Howell had it towed to Islip, Long Island, for cleaning and repairs. The bowsprit was rebuilt, the decks stripped, the walls scrubbed and painted. Looking into a hidden compartment, Howell found items missed by the pirate and the police: a black valise with clothes, a knife, and a manifest dated March 15, 1860, that listed the names and particulars of the crew:

- GEO. H. BURR, master, Islip, L.I., aged 39 years, height 5 feet 6 3/4 inches.
- WM. JOHNSON, first hand, New-York, aged 42 years, height 6 feet 1 inch, wages $19 per month, advance $8.
- OLIVER WATTS, seaman, Islip, L.I., aged 23 years, height 5 feet 7 inches, wages $18.
- SMITH WATTS, cook and hand, Islip, L.I., aged 19 years, height 5 feet 11 inches, wages $16.

Only Johnson had not put his signature beside his name; he left an X.

An affidavit supplied by Ben Nickerson, captain of the *J. R. Mather,* the ship that spoiled Hicks's getaway, was read to the jury and into the court record. Nickerson, who'd been waylaid by weather—he missed the entire trial—described the collision in exact detail. He said it took him by complete surprise, the ghost sloop appearing as if from nowhere: the splintering wood, a sickening sound for a seafaring man, the rope and rigging raining down. Nickerson gave this gear to Captain Weed, who later identified it as belonging to the *E. A. Johnson.* A beam from the wreckage fit the bowsprit of the *Johnson* like a puzzle piece. Nickerson saw no lights on the other ship, but he did spot a man at the rail, or thought he did, a dark figure in a long coat. Nickerson called to the man but got no answer. He was there for just a moment, then was gone.

Next to testify was Daniel Simmons, the wholesaler who'd given Captain Burr the money to buy the oysters. He'd handed over the silver and gold coins in the same bag Hicks had later been seen carrying across Staten Island. Simmons said he'd first noticed Hicks working on the deck of the *E. A. Johnson* at the Spring Street pier, then again at Gravesend Bay. "His whiskers had been full and red," said Simmons. "They're darker now." Simmons was one of the first men to walk through the *Johnson* after it was towed into the Fulton Fish Market pier. Asked to describe the scene, he said, "There was as much blood as if a bullock had been killed. On the rail was a cut, as though a man had clinched hold there and been cut off."

That first day of the trial was devastating for the defense, but Hicks did not seem to notice. His mood was ebullient when he left the courthouse. He walked beside Captain Rynders, who, in his neat blue uniform and black boots, was surrounded by deputies in the way of a politician or celebrity. It meant something to be in the marshal's company. His voice rang above the din.

Hicks hardly spoke. If he did, it was about unimportant things, "trifling topics," according to the *Post*. "He said he feared the plaster of Paris [that P. T. Barnum would use] in taking a cast of his features for Barnum's museum would make him appear pale. Today he thought the audience [in court had] looked like a parcel of fools and in response to some applications made him in regard his name, declared that he would tell nothing without being well paid for it."

The trial would continue for six days—a week of courthouse time. In those six days, the waste was made plain to the jury: three stolen lives, the money they'd never make, trips untaken, children unborn. As it said in the Talmud, "Whoever destroys a soul, it is considered as if he destroyed an entire world." The crimes and the night of the crimes, black water beneath a black sky, the ax blade and severed fingers, the moon rising above a jagged coast—the chain of evidence, each clue, each twisted link, led back to the bad man, whose history was mysterious, whose purpose was cold and inexplicable. Together the twenty-seven witnesses would create a mosaic, each painting his or her own little picture, and each little picture contributing to a terrible design.

The newspapers described all of them, but a few stood out:

Reuben Keymer, who'd seen Hicks at Gravesend Bay before the *Johnson* set out on its last voyage. He'd looked at Hicks, met his eye, turned away. "I was afraid he would run afoul of me." Later, "I watched the sloop going out," Keymer said. "She went southwest to clear Coney Island, then took a southerly course. I saw her three miles out to the east of Sandy Hook."

Samuel Stevens, captain of the *Ceres,* the tug that pushed the wounded sloop across the harbor. He'd reached the *Johnson* at six-thirty A.M., boarded her, walked the decks, and gone down to the cabin, which "appeared as if someone had been slaughtered."

Hart Weed, captain of the second precinct. He'd been shocked by what he'd seen on the sloop. The cabin looked as if someone had tried to wash it down. He found a broom and a bucket. He found bore holes near the floor and the auger that made those holes.

Theodore Burdett of Harbor Patrol, who found the missing yawl on Staten Island, in the tall grass near the beach.

Abram Egbert, who worked at Vanderbilt's ferry terminal on Staten Island. He'd seen Hicks coming up Richmond Road with a bag on his shoulder.

Francis McCaffrey, the cabin boy on the *Southfield* who'd been "brooming" the hallway when Hicks called him into the ladies' cabin at seven A.M. "He asked if I was a good judge of this country's money." McCaffrey described what Hicks had been wearing, the monkey coat and the Kossuth hat. The prosecutor told Hicks to put on the coat so McCaffrey could be sure it was the same man.

Judge Smalley told Hicks he was under no obligation, but Hicks did so anyway, pulling the coat on with languid ease. McCaffrey stared at him for a moment, then said, "That's the boy"—a remark that caused everyone in the courtroom to laugh, even the accused.

William Drumm, the sixteen-year-old urchin who'd carried Hicks's bag from South Ferry to the corner of Greenwich and Cedar streets. Drumm had asked for fifty cents. Hicks gave him three shillings, saying, "Now get, or I'll kick you."

Each witness offered a different view of the same character: a harried sailor on the lam, manic, with a wild look in his eyes, tired but elated, pumped full of air, stingy, generous, wanting to buy a drink for the house, explaining the cause of his good fortune again and again but each time in a different way.

When Elias Smith took the stand, he told the jury about his role as a reporter in the manhunt, and about how he'd confronted the fugitive in the Providence jail: "I said, 'Hicks, you are charged with the murder of three men.' He said nothing. I then changed the language and said, 'You are charged with imbruing your hands in the blood of three of your fellow men for money.' He exhibited no particular surprise, but just shook his head, saying, 'I don't know nothing about it.'"

Detective Nevins described the arrest, Hicks hiding under the blankets, all that sweat. Searching Hicks's rooms, he found money and Captain Burr's watch, among other things. "I told him he was charged with passing counterfeit," said Nevins. "He said he got the money from his brother, and afterwards that he was a speculator in the market, and got the money that way."

Nevins talked about escorting Hicks back to New York on the train, how he read Hicks a newspaper story about the murders, how Hicks turned away, saying, "I know nothing about it."

"You'll be identified in New York," Nevins told him.

"You are free to think whatever you like," said Hicks.

The watch found on Hicks was shown to the jury. Each man studied it, then passed it along. The prosecutor called the watchmaker Samuel Conover to the stand. His shop at 182 Bowery was frequented by sailors. Examining the piece, Conover said, "I remember repairing [this] about a year ago for a person named Burr, 6th April, 1859. It was a doubled-cased silver watch. The makers' name J. Johnson and the number was 21,310."

Tension grew as the days went by—disgust turned to fascination, a strange electric atmosphere building toward a climax. "As this trial approaches its termination, the interest of the public seems to increase," the *Times* reported on May 19, 1860. "There were not more people inside the Court-room yesterday than on the day previous, for that would have been impossible, but a great many more tried to get in than on any former occasion, and went away disappointed."

Hicks sailed above it all, oblivious, detached. Given the circumstances, perhaps it was the best course, better than bitching and protesting, weeping or breaking down. He was living his last days like an Existentialist—enjoying the moment as long as there was a moment to enjoy, savoring the dregs as you'd savor a first sip. What was the difference, really? At the Tombs, he was allowed to bathe a few times a week. His kept his beard neatly trimmed. In court, he dressed as if for a funeral—his own—in a dark coat and black tie, a suit provided by the Masons. He sat calmly at the defense table, listening but far away, as if taking it all in from a distance.

The prosecution saved its most dramatic witnesses for the end of the trial, the third and fourth day. These were men and women, some intimately involved with the victims, who could connect Hicks to the crime via the most common elements of life—hair and clothes. A shudder went through the court when the prosecutor called Catherine Dickenson, Oliver Watts's seventeen-year-old girlfriend. The jurors knew her face; they'd seen it in the daguerreotype that Hicks had been carrying when arrested. Miss Dickenson, who lived in Brooklyn, told the court she'd last seen Oliver "on the Tuesday of the week he sailed. I gave him my daguerreotype. . . . He put it in his coat pocket."

She said the picture had been part of a pair—one of her for him, one of him for her. She was still wearing hers in a locket around her neck. When she took it off and showed it to the court—a young man with handsome features—people in the gallery were anguished. Some cried. She opened the locket and removed the picture. Behind it were a few locks from Oliver's head. "I cut his hair," she explained. "I did it once a month. It grew so quickly."

The strands were given to the jurors, who examined them next to some hair found in the blood on the deck of the sloop. This side-by-side study was about as close as you got to forensic analysis in 1860. The hair apparently came from the same person. Asked her opinion, Miss

Dickerson said, "It's indeed from Oliver. I knew every hair on his head. I knew it better than he knew it himself."

Then Dideme Burr, the captain's widow, was called. She'd left the hospital a few days before and insisted on testifying. She was pale and wore black. The newspapers described her attire as "deep mourning." She identified the watch that had been found on Hicks—the tarnished timepiece her husband had carried for nine years and consulted constantly.

Abbey Hubbard, the mother of Smith Watts, had testified earlier but was recalled, making her the last witness. When she spoke of her younger son, the tenderness and clarity of it crushed the people in the gallery. Many wept. She said Smith had only been nineteen at the time of his death, slender, with skinny arms and wrists. He did not yet shave. He was too trusting, easy prey in a cruel world. His father had run off years before—perhaps Smith thought he'd find him out there in the world. The boy had lived in Islip with his mother and the man she had married, Mr. Hubbard. She had at first refused to let Smith go to sea, but there was no holding him. She insisted on outfitting him before he left, so he would at least be warm. Over the course of several days, she made an entire wardrobe, "a blue woolen shirt . . . two pair of pantaloons sewn by candlelight." The clothes were found in Hicks's rooms in Providence. They were shown to Mrs. Hubbard, who led a kind of tour of each item. "I patched this shirt myself," she said. "[And] this bag has the initials of my present husband, Lorenzo Hubbard. I put my son's clothes in that morning. I knew the shirts. . . . I cut them in the old fashion way myself. I have had no tidings of him since, only that I suppose he was murdered."

The prosecution closed its case on a Thursday morning. During a recess, Hicks could be seen talking to Captain Rynders, who was amid a crowd, telling jokes. Then it was time for the defense attorney, Sayles, to make his case. He called just two witnesses—Kenneth White and Edward Barnes, who lauded the prisoner's work ethic but had nothing important to contribute. In truth, there was no good defense. Instead, Sayles tried to poke holes in the state's case. He did not have to prove Hicks innocent, he reminded the jury, nor discover who committed the crimes. He merely had to create doubt, open a shaft for light to come in. Jurors don't want to hang a person— that's a stain you carry forever. The defense must merely give them a reason not to.

On the last day, Sayles tried to accomplish this in his closing argument, making several points, hoping that one would do the trick. For starters, he said, the court should not be hearing the case at all—it was a misreading of the piracy statute, which was unconstitutional and would eventually be struck down. According to that unsound law, the crime of piracy, to be heard in this court, must occur on the high seas—which it most assuredly did not, the Lower Bay being no less a part of New York City than the Bowery. *We should be in a* New York *court, before a* New York *judge,* Sayles explained. He "cited from numerous law-books, authorities to sustain his position," the *Times* reported. "The United States Court, not being a Court of common law jurisdiction, the prisoner could not be convicted of any minor degree of the offence charged, as he could be in a Court of common law; yet, if they (the prosecution) failed to prove it was committed on the high seas, it was an offence punishable by common law, and necessarily should go to the State Courts."

Judge Smalley dismissed this argument, telling the jury it did indeed have jurisdiction, which pushed Sayles on to his second point: the accused could not receive a fair hearing in this courtroom on account of the "incredible amount of interest and press this case received before the accused even stood before a judge." All the attention and anger of the city had been directed at this one man. *Well, I've got a question,* said Sayles. *What if he didn't do it? How can the jury, having been soaked in a great flood of publicity, not look at him as a killer before the case even began?*

Judge Smalley dismissed this argument too, pushing Sayles on to his third point: the case presented by the prosecution was entirely circumstantial. The prosecutor, James Dwight, had identified and marked a man for death based on a handful of physical items that yes, might have been on the sloop—let's accept that they were— which did not mean the sloop was where the defendant got those items, the world being filled with secondhand sailor junk. Sayles suggested the jurors take a look in the stalls of the Washington Market before they send his client to the next world. "Looks bad" does not mean "Is bad," he explained. There was simply not enough evidence to "fasten guilt upon my client, or to show that he did not honestly come by" these items. Perhaps these crimes were committed by river pirates, whom the police told us were in action the same night. They robbed another ship in the vicinity of the *E. A. Johnson,* as Harbor

Patrol could tell you. Maybe Oliver Watts stumbled across the Daybreak Boys or the Swamp Angels as they were raiding the *Johnson,* and they silenced him and the rest of the crew. Or maybe the killings were done by someone else altogether—how can we really know?

Sayles spoke of past cases in which defendants, identified, tried, convicted, were later shown to be innocent. What about the murder of that New England postman? Dozens of people had identified a man as the killer, but he was later cleared. What if he'd been executed before he'd been exonerated? Or the Bourne brothers, accused and convicted in the killing of a Mr. Colvin in Vermont in 1819—the brothers had actually confessed, been sentenced, and were awaiting execution when the real killer came forward. "But the most astonishing thing about the prosecution is the charge that this one man should kill these three men, powerful as they were, and not receive a single scratch," Sayles told the jury. "There must have been a terrible struggle. Blood was spattered over the ceiling, blood everywhere, but [there was] no blood on him, no mark of violence on his person."

Did that sound possible?

Think before you decide, he said. *Consider all the circumstances. A man can be put to death, but he cannot be brought back.*

It was the prosecution's turn to close. The gallery was filled with reporters for the occasion, attorneys, court officers, sailors, friends of the dead—it was the best kind of theater. "Hicks sat coolly and even coldly at the defense table, looking down, twisting a pen in his hand," according to one newspaper account. "He would not make eye contact with the jurors."

Did Hicks still believe in escape?

There was that silver train again, highballing across the evening sky.

James Dwight stood before the jury. He would live to be an old man, see the assassination of Lincoln and the triumph of the railroad, but this was the biggest audience and biggest moment he would ever know. "I had hoped the defense would prove me wrong and prove this man innocent of these crimes, but I have been disappointed," he told the jury.

> "The defense has contradicted not one fact or witness that the state has presented. That means all these things had to happen by coincidence and chance. The defense would endeavor to induce the jury to believe that Captain Burr parted with his watch, which he had carried for nine years, to a pawnbroker; that Smith Watts had parted with the clothes which his aged mother had put up for him; that Oliver Watts had parted with the daguerreotype of the girl he loved. The time has not yet come when Yankee sailor boys give up pictures of the girls they left behind without a struggle."

Dwight spoke to the jurors as you might speak to a friend at the end of a particularly bad day.

> "Gentlemen, I have occupied your time longer than I intended," he said, "and I have but one

word further to say. If this prisoner is not proven guilty of the crime against him, he is of course an innocent man. If there is in the breast of any of you one doubt concerning his guilt—one reasonable doubt as to his having committed this robbery of George H. Burr, as set forth in the indictment, in God's name give him the benefit of that doubt. It is his sacred privilege, and it is just as much his right as he has a right to his life or his liberty. If you have any doubt upon considering the evidence, give him the benefit of that doubt, or any which you may have.

"But if you think him guilty. . . .

"Here, in your very seats, I charge you to give the benefit of your conviction to the government, and I charge you to do this in your jury box without any hesitation. Gentlemen, there was no hesitation on his part: with that sharp ax he cut down the fair-haired boy, Watts; and then returned and felled the other; and then the death struggle with the captain occurred. Gentlemen, there was no hesitation there; and if you are convinced of his guilt, let there be no hesitation in your rendering in your jury box a verdict against him. There cries from the sands of Islip, 'justice;' from that widow and from that mother. There comes up 'from the depths of the Atlantic, from all the ships that float on it, and all that go down in the great deep'— there comes the cry of 'justice.' The prisoner equally calls on you to do justice; and gentlemen, I ask you, in the name of the government, if you believe him guilty of this crime, which he committed speedily, summarily and devilishly, that you will let your verdict be speedy, summary and just."

It was four P.M. on Thursday, May 17, 1860.

Judge Smalley made a final statement to the jury on Saturday. "The Court room was excessively crowded, but profound silence prevailed during the delivery of the charge," the *Times* reported. "The prisoner listened to it attentively. His appearance was somewhat haggard, indicating a failure of physical power, and he had lost the nonchalance which he wore at the commencement of the trial."

The jury was sent to deliberate at 10:36 A.M. How long does it take one man to kill another? How long does it take a body, thrown overboard, to reach the bottom of the bay? How long does it take a soul to ascend to heaven? The jury came back after seven minutes. At 10:43 A.M., the judge told the foreman, James Fuller, to stand. Albert Hicks stood and faced him.

"Have you reached a verdict?" asked Judge Smalley.

"We have," said Fuller.

What is it?

We the people find the defendant guilty of piracy on the high seas.

Hicks fell back into the chair and closed his eyes. "Otherwise," according to the *Times,* "except for a nervous twitching of the fingers, he made no sign indicative of the position in which the verdict of the Jury had placed him."

Rynders dropped a rough hand onto Hicks's shoulder. The condemned held out his wrists to be shackled. Sayles rushed the bench, shouting at the judge, saying he'd ask for a new trial. Judge Smalley nodded.

That case was made and rejected a few days later.

All the relevant parties, along with dozens of reporters, were back in the courtroom the following week to hear the sentence. It was no surprise. The prosecution charged piracy specifically because the fate of a pirate is so well established.

Smalley made the most of the moment even so: "It is now my duty, and my painful duty as an officer of the United States, to move for the judgment which the law has affixed as a punishment to the crime of piracy upon the high seas in the case of Albert Hicks," he told the court.

> The prisoner has been found guilty of the crime and to that the law assigned the punishment of death, and no other punishment. It has left no discretion to the Court, as there is none with the jury or the District-Attorney. Were it an ordinary case I should make this application with great pain. Capital punishments are not favorites with me, nor with the community; and for the crime of robbery on the high seas, dangerous though it may be, if it stood by itself, the feeling of the community would be against inflicting the punishment of death, and would be in this case were it not for the surrounding circumstances. In making this application I do it with the knowledge, for with this verdict before us we have the legal knowledge, as we have also the moral knowledge, that though the charge is

one of piracy, it involves also a charge of the murder of three men in cold blood, for the mere, I had almost said paltry, consideration of $150, some old clothes, and an old watch. Three men have been deprived of their lives, unwarned, probably in the dead of night, when the perpetrator incurred no seeming risk of detection, men who had been his comrades, with whom he had broken bread for days and days—these men were ruthlessly, cruelly and surreptitiously deprived of their lives, and one of them when life enough remained, not to defend himself, but to struggle for life, and while clinging to the side of the vessel and pleading for mercy, had his hand chopped off by the man who had previously murdered his companions. In such a case I should feel authorized to ask for the highest punishment of the law, if the law had provided for any degrees in the punishment of the offence.

Looking at the convict, the judge asked, "Is there any reason why this sentence should not be passed upon you?"

"No," said Hicks, in a whisper. "I have nothing to say."

Smalley nodded, then went on.

You, Albert W. Hicks, otherwise William Johnson, have been indicted by the Grand Jury for this District for robbery and piracy on the high seas. You have had a patient and fair trial before an honest jury of your country. You have been defended by able counsel with zeal and fidelity, but found guilty. The evidence against you was so strong, clear, and conclusive that no one who heard it could doubt as to the correctness of the verdict. The evidence also established beyond a moral or rational doubt that, in order to accomplish the robbery, you were guilty of a triple murder; that to enable you to possess yourself of the paltry sum of $150 in money and some articles of clothing not your own, you, the first officer of the sloop in which you sailed, as she was proceeding to sea, in the stillness of the night, and under its cover, in cold blood and without provocation, murdered three innocent, unoffensive persons, and threw them into the sea; and the next morning attempted escape with your blood-stained plunder. But the finger of Providence seems to have followed you, and pointed you out to the guardians of the law. You were pursued, arrested and most of your ill gotten gains found upon you, and identified by the most unmistakable evidence as the property and clothing of the missing, and as it appeared on the trial, murdered men. The annals of crime present few cases of greater atrocity and horror. For this most inhuman and revolting violation of the laws of your country and of the great Ruler of the universe you must soon and justly pay the forfeit of your life. The crime is of such an aggravated character and your guilt is so certain and incontestable, that you must not hope anything from Executive clemency. The Court, therefore, would urge you to earnestly and sincerely devote the little time that may yet remain to you of life, to repentance and preparing to meet your last and final Judge.

The sentence of the law and the Court is that you be taken from this place to the prison from whence you came, there kept in close confinement until Friday, the 13th day of July next, and on that day taken from thence to Ellis Island or to Bedloe's Island, in the Bay of New-York, as the Marshal for this District may elect, and there, between the hours of 10 o'clock in the morning and 3 o'clock in the afternoon, be hung by the neck until you are dead.

THE CONFESSION

Albert Hicks did not change cells. He was still on the Murderers' Corridor, Cell 8, the Tombs. But his cell took on a new aspect—it had gone from holding tank to death row. Public executions had been discontinued in New York City. Once upon a time, dozens of people had been executed every year before huge crowds in Manhattan. The last such hanging occurred in the spring of 1824, when over fifty thousand people watched the killer John Johnson swing from a gallows on the corner of Second Avenue and Thirteenth Street. But the crowd had been a little too drunk and festive on that occasion. It did not have the desired effect of deterring crime but became a boozy party instead. The executions went on, but for the most part, they were done privately, in the courtyard behind the Tombs.

Hicks was unusual in that he'd been convicted as a pirate in the federal system, hence was destined to hang publicly—he would in fact be the last man publicly executed in New York. Bedloe's Island was chosen because it was federal property as well as a traditional place of execution for buccaneers, standing as it does between the city and the open sea.

Hicks's demeanor changed as soon as the sentence was read. Hearing those words—"hung by the neck till dead"—seemed to unsettle him. Little by little, the mask fell away. According to the prison warden, Hicks wept in his cell in the dead of night. His shoulders shook, and his eyes were red and searching. He'd never believed he'd be caught—"It never even occurred to me," he said. Now he was right up against it, looking the thing square in the face.

Hicks told the warden he wanted to talk to a priest. He had been raised a Catholic—his parents were Irish and German—but it had been years since he'd been in a church. The warden sent a message to the College of St. Francis Xavier on Sixteenth Street. The next morning Father Henry Duranquet stood outside Cell 8. Working with doomed men was the priest's specialty. He was among the last survivors of a legendary family. There were noblemen, bishops, and holy fools among his ancestors. He was born in 1809 in Chalus, in Clermont, France, one of six brothers. Five of them grew up to become priests—*les cinq pères Duranquet*. All were Jesuits. Many died young. The oldest went to the Madura Mission in India, where he spread the good news, wept and prayed, caught cholera, and died at age thirty-seven. The next oldest, Charles, followed to the Madura Mission, carried on weeping and praying, caught cholera, and died at age thirty-nine. Victor, the third brother, died of "hardship and labor" at thirty-three.

Henry, second to youngest, was educated in local academies, then sent to Rome to finish his schooling. He was tall and slight, as reedy as an El Greco saint. After taking his vows in Italy, he was sent to New Orleans. Eighteen thirty-six was a high point in the life of that city—wine-soaked alleys and palm shadows, church bells, ships lining the French Quarter docks. He was seen, even then, as a man of depth. (As Oscar Wilde later said, "We are all in the gutter, but some of us are looking at the stars.") He did sacred work all over the New World, from Louisiana to New York to Quebec. He carried his faith before him like a torch.

In 1851 Father Duranquet was transferred to the College of St. Francis Xavier in Manhattan, where he was to teach, advise, and administer the sacraments. New York was filling with refugees from Germany and Ireland, Catholics who faced prejudice and poverty, crying out from the Five Points and Fourth Ward, a flood of humanity in need of guidance. One day the father volunteered to talk to a man in spiritual crisis on Blackwell's Island (today, as Roosevelt Island, it's crowded with playgrounds and condos), home to a poorhouse, a sanitarium, and a prison. It was a place you tried to avoid, but Father Duranquet went there willingly, even joyfully. He spent hours with the prisoner, leading him from darkness into the light. But it was not the man who struck him so much as the multitude of men, in yards and cages, each soul lost, reaching out for help. If the priest did his work here, amid the lowest, tremendous progress could be made. It was a weedy patch, an untended field. What a few diligent hours could do! It became his specialty: Father Duranquet, the shepherd of the condemned.

He had an ability to reach people who seemed unreachable. A Catholic journal credited his personality; helpfully, he was a little dumb. His brain didn't get in the way; nor was he distracted by minutiae. He focused on the big things, on eternity and damnation. Prisoners, used to being ignored, mistreated, or turned into symbols, experienced his attention as an elixir and a revelation. "A remarkable characteristic of all Duranquet's work was his calm, deliberate way," according to the Catholic journal. He "often seemed to the younger men too slow, but, while those of greater energy wore themselves out and met an early death, our good father continued on and thus did more in reality by his slowness and the great experience he had gained, than those who would do everything at once."

That first morning Father Duranquet sat with Albert Hicks for several hours, side by side on the straw mattress, a guard looking in through the bars. We can't know what they discussed or what passed between them, but based on the priest's religious philosophy and considering how Hicks began to change soon afterward, we can guess.

Albert Hicks knew he was trapped. He'd believed he could get out of this trap, as he'd got out of every other, as his brother had done. He said it several times. There would be a legal loophole, or he'd escape. His brother was the shining example—Simon had been in the same fix and was now a free man out west. But the words of the judge ate through his mind like a worm—*"hung by the neck till dead."* Nonchalance turned to concern, then fear, then panic. One night Hicks asked the warden to sit with him. He said he was scared to be alone.

Father Duranquet promised him a different kind of escape: to the next world. As Hicks came to accept the inevitability of his execution, his attention turned to God, not an abstract god of nature but the Old Testament God, a man on a throne in the sky. Hicks knew he was going to hell for his actions. In fact, in the days after the verdict, he focused his anger on the devil. He believed he'd made a deal with the devil, and as part of that deal, the devil was supposed to protect him from capture. He now felt betrayed. If the devil had quit him, then couldn't he quit the devil? That's what he wanted to know from the priest. Was it too late to switch sides, get with the righteous, and win a place for himself in the heavenly kingdom?

It's never too late, said Father Duranquet. *Not as long as you're living. You need only open your heart and accept Jesus Christ.* Hicks had been the worst kind of sinner, which meant he had a lot of work to do. He had to do it inside himself. He must admit his crimes, confess, and beg forgiveness. And it must all be genuine and real. It would be hard. Hicks had taught himself over the years never to admit or tell the truth, because once you did, you'd be finished. They wanted confessions, he thought, not to forgive or rehabilitate or understand people like himself, but to feel righteous when they strung him up.

Father Duranquet visited Hicks every day. He spent a part of each morning in Cell 8, talking to, listening to, or praying with the prisoner. An emotional bond formed. People noticed it and its effect on the prisoner. "Hicks seemed to lose that firmness which he had hitherto manifested," Lorenzo De Angelis, a deputy marshal who spent hours with the prisoner, said later. "His reckless indifference left him, and in place of the stolid look which had marked his face from the time of his arrest an appearance of deep anxiety gave token that he had abandoned the hope which had supported him, and that dread of his approaching fate, if not remorse for his crimes, had taken possession of him."

Hints of the coming confession can first be seen in an interview Hicks gave the *Times* in June 1860.

THE MURDERS ON THE OYSTER SLOOP

A Partial Confession from Hicks
He Admits His Guilt and Details Some of
the Particulars of the Tragedy

"Hicks, I have formed a theory of the manner in which Capt. BURR, and the WATTS boys were murdered, and I believe it was done between the hours of 12 o'clock at night and 3 in the morning."

"No," replied HICKS, "they killed them between 9 and 10 o'clock at night."

"What do you mean by they?" rejoined his questioner. "There were but four men on board the sloop, and you were one of the four. I am surprised at your attempt to deceive me, HICKS, and shall have nothing further to do with you, if you treat me in that way."

"But there were five on board," said HICKS, with a cunning smile. "The devil was the fifth personage; he possessed me and urged me on to do it. You see, I was at the helm, and one of the WATTS was forward on the lookout, while Capt. BURR and the other lad were asleep below. I had entertained the idea of murdering them for some time, and the devil kept telling me now was the chance. I walked forward quietly, and before the young man was aware of my intentions, I dealt him a tremendous blow on the head. He fell down, but I had to repeat the blow several times before I could kill him. Meantime the noise and scuffling woke up the man who was sleeping in the hold, and just as he got on deck I struck him. He wasn't so hard to dispatch as the first one."

Q.—"What sort of an instrument did you use? Was it a marlin spike or hand-spike?"

This question HICKS could not be induced to answer, merely replying that it was a heavy instrument. His manner and subsequent remarks conveyed the impression to the mind of his questioner that an axe was the weapon he had used.

HICKS resumed—"After I had finished the boys, I went to the cabin and found Capt. BURR just coming upon deck. He asked what the matter was, and I struck at him. He's a mighty powerful man, and he attempted to grapple me, and it was a long time before I could overpower him. I brought him at last," he added triumphantly.

"Oh! the resistance of the Captain accounts for the marks of the terrific struggle in the cabin; the wood-work was hacked as if with an axe, and there was a great quantity of blood about."

To this remark HICKS assented, and the gentleman went on—

"But there were bloody finger-marks on the

gunwale, and you must have thrown one of them overboard before he was dead, and while he was clinging to the side, chopped his fingers off."

"No, Sir; they had all been dead more than an hour when I pitched them over," said HICKS. He then said: "They tell me one of the bodies has been found; is it true?"

"I believe so," was the reply.

"Well, I don't; you see, when all this happened we were fifty miles from Sandy Hook, and I took care their graves should be deep—very deep."

He was then asked what his feelings could have been, alone as he was on the vessel, with nothing to be seen but the stars above him and the wide waters around him, while his shipmates, murdered by his hand, lay mutilated and bleeding on the deck?

"Oh!" said he, "it makes me shudder now, but then I did not mind it. I told you the devil urged me on; he sustained me then, but now he has deserted me."

Hicks asked the warden and the deputy marshal to meet him in his cell. He'd been with the priest all morning, weeping and praying, holding and kissing the Bible, which he could not read. He said he'd come to a decision. He wanted to confess, tell the story of his crimes—not just the murders on the *E. A. Johnson* but all the murders. Not just on this ghost ship but on all the ghost ships. He wanted to tell the story of his life. It would turn out to be remarkable. More than the story of a single ruined man, it was the story of the underworld and the waterfront, oceans and tides, frontier towns and seaports, the Old West and the modern metropolis, the South Pacific and the Horn of Africa, gun smoke and gold strikes, the wildest parts of the hemisphere. It was Yankee enterprise deformed by rage, blood-soaked and shot full of holes. It was America as seen in a funhouse mirror.

Hicks told it in the course of one long morning. He said he was doing it for his wife and child. They were impoverished. The confession would help, as he would sing for whomever was willing to pay most, which turned out to be New York publisher R. M. De Witt, whose typical titles included *The Highwayman's Bride; or, the Capture of Claude Duval; Clog Dancing Made Easy;* and *Revelations of a Slave Smuggler: Being the Autobiography of Capt. Rich'd Drake, An African Trader for Fifty Years—From 1807 to 1857.* De Witt, headquartered at 33 Rose Street, would release Hicks's book on the morning of the execution. According to one account, the prisoner asked for his fee in coins—he said he did not trust "the folding kind"—in hopes of bludgeoning his way to freedom with sacks of silver, but this story was a typical rumor. The man who took the confession, Deputy Marshal Lorenzo De Angelis—he worked at the command of Isaiah Rynders and was partnered with the transcriber G. W. Clackner—swore in a letter to the *Times* that the whole thing had been straightforward. "Every cent of the money realized from the sale of the confession will be applied to the use of the widow and the child," De Angelis wrote, "and the wretched man will have the satisfaction of knowing that he does not leave them entirely destitute and dependent on the charity of the world."

To Hicks, the confession was about more than money—it was about eternal life. The way is narrow, the priest had explained to him, and if Hicks hoped to travel it, he must tell what he had done, and not just what he felt like telling but all of it. He did so on July 9, 1860, four days before hanging. He was in Cell 8, amid a few spellbound people, speaking in a singsong pirate patois full of waterfront lingo. No one had ever heard him talk at length—he had usually uttered no more than two or three sentences at a time, as few words as absolutely necessary. They now realized he was in fact an accomplished talker and a garrulous raconteur.

Deputy Marshal De Angelis said the confession was taken down "as nearly as possible, word for word as it came out of the mouth of Hicks," but reading it, you can tell it was edited and otherwise finessed by someone at the publishing house. The prose is ornate, high-flown, and Victorian, American literary writing as it was before the simplifying purities of Lincoln and Hemingway— fancy, baroque, spritzed with perfume, ten-cent words and the sort of wraparound sentences that a man like Hicks, a man of barrooms and ships, would never have spoken. It is, for example, impossible to imagine the killer saying, "I look back upon my way of life, and see the path marked with blood and crime, and, in the still midnight, if I sleep, I act the dreadful scenes anew." His actual language was overwritten and lost. We can imagine it—we vaguely know how sailors spoke in the 1850s— but never recover it. What we have instead are the underlying facts, the skeletal bones of the epic story.

The senselessness of the killings aboard the *E. A. Johnson*—that was what terrified people. One hundred fifty dollars, an old watch, two pairs of pantaloons, and a picture of a pretty girl he would never meet—was that really what it was all about, was that really why three innocents had to meet such a terrible fate? That motive was a pill the public could not swallow.

Hicks fixed that problem in the first moments of his confession. Yes, the motive had been money, he said, but also something more. It was what had driven him to do most of the terrible things he had done in his forty years of life: his desire for revenge on the world. He wanted everyone to feel just as woebegone and forsaken and damned to hell as he did.

Albert Hicks was born in 1820 in Foster, Rhode Island, the youngest member of a large family, the sixth of seven sons, meaning, according to folklore, he was marked by a blessing or a curse. His father was a farmer who was often said to be honest, which seems less a statement of fact than a critique of the son. *Why can't you be more like* . . . Albert's first memories were of fields—red in summer; green in spring; white in winter; gold in fall—that rose and fell around the house like a heaving sea.

He had been unruly even when small, the kind of boy you're warned to keep at a distance. "I was naturally of a wild, restless, reckless disposition, fonder of wandering about the fields, or lounging by the brook side, than following the habits of industry," he told De Angelis. He got into fights constantly, set off by the merest provocation. Not many children battle as if they intend to do real harm. He did, and it made him feared. He'd take his first shot at a boy's face and end it right there. He was always getting the paddle or the strap, the back of the hand. His father wanted him to work on the farm, but it was soon clear that he did not have the temperament. He wandered off when given even a small task. You'd find the hoe in the field and the boy gone, the forest lurking all around. "My only ambition was to be rich," Hicks said, "but I had no desire to acquire riches in the plodding way in which our neighbors went through life; my dream was to become suddenly rich by some bold stroke, and then to give free reins to the passions that governed me."

He was trained in shoemaking and carpentry—his father insisted on it, knowing the boy, a son of his old age, would need a trade to survive in the world. But it was not shoe-making or carpentry that got Albert dreaming. It was treasure. "I used to wish I could find pots of gold and silver which rumor said had been buried in our neighborhood by pirates and robbers," he explained. "I used to listen with rapt attention to stories of pirates, robbers, highwaymen."

The Rhode Island shore had long been rank with buccaneers—it was a famous privateer coast. Captain Thomas Paine, who sailed under a black flag out of Jamestown, Virginia, drove the French from Block Island and led a raid on St. Augustine, capital of Spanish Florida. Captain Kidd, the notorious British pirate who buried some of his treasure on Gardiner's Island in Long Island Sound and some on Bedloe's Island, where Hicks was to be hung, sailed his ten-gun ship, the *St. Antonio,* into Narragansett Bay in 1699, where he found refuge. This golden age of criminality lasted until 1723, when twenty-six pirates were hung on Gravelly Point off Long

Wharf in Newport, Rhode Island, perhaps the largest public execution in U.S. history.

Hicks was raised on these stories as later gangsters would be raised on stories of Hicks. They set his mind adrift, filled him with wanderlust. He had some savings from work doing errands and odd jobs. At fifteen, he took this money and ran away—lit out across the fields, his shadow stretching before him. He headed for the biggest place he knew, Providence, Rhode Island, which occupied a commanding position on Narragansett harbor, a gateway to the sea. Nearly fifty thousand people lived in Providence. There were taverns and boardinghouses, there were immigrant-choked streets. Hicks hung around the waterfront dives, amid tattooed men.

He stayed till his money was gone, then went to Norwich, Connecticut, where he hoped to get a job. When he was still living with his family, they used to visit Norwich on market days—his father sold the autumn harvest there. The elder Hicks was, as a result, known in Norwich, a buzzing country town near the confluence of the Yantic, the Shetucket, and the Quinebaug rivers. Hicks walked in and out of the shops, skulked around the mills and the factories, looked for work and was chased away. If he had caught his reflection in a window, he would have seen a brooding adolescent, dark-eyed and oversize, with handsome features and the beginnings of a beard.

After two days, he was hungry. He went into the train station. People were coming and going amid the shrill whistle of engines and early morning traffic. He noticed luggage set against the station wall to be transferred to connecting trains. He returned that night, picked up a bag, and walked out. He carried it into the woods, then went back and got another. He found little of value in these bags: clothes, a book, a lady's underthings. He kept the underthings and traded the rest. He later said he'd swapped it with a peddler for bread and a few coins.

All told, he was gone less than a week. He must have suffered his return as a defeat. His parents demanded to know where he'd been, but he wouldn't say, or did say but his story was unbelievable, or did say but his story kept changing. Meanwhile the thefts had been reported in Norwich. The police made inquiries. Several people remembered seeing young Hicks hanging around the station. The police turned up at the farm in the middle of the night. They went into the boy's room, woke him, and searched his things. They found the coins and underwear. He was arrested and taken to jail. He would, in a sense, never make it back home. He was leaving as one kind of person—reckless but innocent—and would return as another kind.

He was tried and convicted in the town court. Not yet sixteen, he was sentenced to eighteen months in Norwich prison. It was 1835. To be a boy in a nineteenth-century penitentiary, in a cold germ-filled lockup, buggered and beaten, the plaything of grown men, was a variety of damnation. He changed in that prison. Whatever soft thing had remained bled away. He became mean. Otherwise he would not have survived. After three months, he saw an opportunity: a key in a lock, an unchained door. He slipped away—became an escaped convict, a dangerous man at large, at loose in the world.

He gamboled across open country, slept in the woods, shed his prison outfit for clothes he found drying on a line. He made it to Glocester, Rhode Island, twenty miles outside Providence. He got a job on a farm, working in fields so much like those of his father, it could make you question the very nature of time. He was there six weeks before he was recognized and sent back to prison.

His sentence was extended. He was beaten, then put to work on the road beside the prison's most hardened convicts. As in the Hank Williams tune, he wore a ball and a chain; a number, not a name. "I had been at work a month in this way, when one day, by means of a stone hammer and chisel, I broke the chain from my leg, and made for the woods, pursued for some miles by a strong party of officers," Hicks told De Angelis. "I took refuge in a house by the roadside, and had the satisfaction of seeing [the guards] go by at full speed, supposing me to be still ahead of them."

He hid in the forest, ate berries, and drank from streams. The next day, thinking he was in the clear, he headed for Providence. A man could lose himself in that city, change his clothes, change his name, never be seen again. He almost made it but not quite. Some busybody along the way spotted him in prison clothes. This man was on horseback. He called to the fugitive, who took one look and ran. He was soon among the trees. The man gave chase, hollering, raising a general alarm. The man came close and dismounted. Hicks knocked him to the ground. They rolled in the muck. "We had a long and terrible struggle in the mud and the water of the swamp," said Hicks, "he all the time shouting at the top of his voice for assistance, which brought the neighbors to his aid before I could effect my determination to kill him."

Hicks was soon back in prison. Bloodied, beaten

black and blue. What had been an eighteen-month sentence was now two years. There'd be no more outside work for him, not on the road crew, not even breaking rocks in the quarry. When you have a bird that flies, take no chances. They put him in a hole, where he had to sit and think. He said he spent an entire year in solitary confinement, closed up with nothing but his increasingly crazy thoughts. He said he went insane in those months, lost all semblance of his old personality. He became fixated on one thing: how unfair life had been to him—he was spending a year in a hole, two in a cage, for what? For stealing a few shirts and a pair of underwear. That was when he changed. That was when he took on the qualities that allowed him, years later, to tell a roomful of reporters, "Who am I? I am the worst man who ever lived." That was when he developed the motive that explained the murders on the *E. A. Johnson*. The world had declared war on Albert Hicks, so Albert Hicks would declare war on the world. He would make the people of the world feel as hopeless and abandoned as he felt in that hole.

Hicks made a classic mistake. He believed that bad luck had befallen only him, that he had been singularly cursed and thus was singularly entitled to revenge. In truth, bad luck befalls everyone all the time. Everyone Hicks would meet on the road was engaged in a fight for their life, but he did not care enough to see it. The few times he did are the few times he showed mercy. But mostly he considered his situation to be unique. He was rough and raw, a brand-new soul.

When Hicks was released in 1837, he went to his father's house but could find no work in the area. He had

the mark of the convict on him, which made him a kind of outcast. He continued on to Glocester, where he got a job making shoes. Stitch the sole, hammer the heel, stand in the yard looking over the roofs of town. He did this for six or seven months. It wasn't the desire for revenge that sent him roaming, but an even more basic engine— boredom. The world is big, and Glocester is small. Perhaps he remembered his childhood dreams of pirate treasure, rubies.

So away to the port of Warren, Rhode Island, where he joined the crew of the whaling ship *Philip Tabb*. He was on deck the night the ship left the harbor. He had been on river ferries, but this was different—a great ship under sail, a whaler bound for distant seas. He was headed to the Pacific, which, in the days before the Panama Canal, meant a long cruise down the Atlantic Coast, then through the Strait of Magellan. He would have seen New York and Charleston on this first voyage, St. Augustine, Nassau, Barranquilla, Caracas, Fortaleza, Rio de Janeiro, Porto Alegre, Puerto Deseado, Rio Gallegos, Punta Arenas, Guayaquil, Acapulco, San Francisco, Seattle— months at sea, with only the occasional port of call for food, water, and a night in the taverns.

In the 1840s the whaling industry was booming, arguably the most important business in America, supplying raw material for half a dozen other industries and, crucially, supplying the oil that kept the cities aglow. For sailors, life on a whaler meant months or even years at sea, circling the globe in pursuit of great schools of bowhead, fin, humpback, narwhal, and gray. But a sperm whale, which might measure sixty feet and weigh fifty tons, was the big prize. It took a strange company of men

to thrive on a whaler—fortune seekers, ne'er-do-wells, ocean lovers, fugitives. Many, like Hicks, were running away, looking to get lost.

Each hand had a unique purpose. The captain set the course; the lookout sat in the crow's nest, scanning for shadows; the harpooner chased the whale in a launch, then drove in the spike, the death dart; the butcher cut the blubber and boiled it down; the helmsman steered. Hicks served mostly as a carpenter, doing odd jobs, making repairs. Like everyone else, he worked for a cut of the take. The captain got one-eighth. A man who worked before the mast got much less. Hicks might expect to get about a one three-hundredth share of the final profit. Which explains the up-and-down mood on such vessels.

When the crew got a whale, everyone was happy and felt rich and acted like brothers. But if the ship went a month with no sightings, the crew turned restless and mean, and all bonds dissolved, and there was talk of mutiny. Most crew members were less like traditional sailors than like workingmen, or modern-day teamsters. If put in charge of a ship, they would not be able to command it—they would drift and die. But they had their own kind of power. These ships were too big to be sailed by just the officers— there might be sixty men on a crew. If half refused to work, the same fate would result: drift and die. In other words, a whaler was society in miniature. Management had the workers by the throat, and workers had management the same. Only the owners, back in their beds at home, awaiting news of profit, were safe.

After that first voyage, Hicks went on dozens of oth-

ers, not just on whalers but on sloops, clippers, merchant traders, fishing boats—whoever was hiring. He made repairs, hauled in sails, sorted the catch, kept watch. He was young, skilled, and strong. Did he take those first jobs with the intention of revolt? Was piracy his aim from the start, part of his general desire for revenge? Or did he go in search of adventure, only to change plans in moments of rage? He was a diligent crewman right up to the instant he flipped. Anything could set him off. Harsh words spoken by the captain, an insult or a superior look, an imagined slight—a man looking to be insulted will be insulted. Or perhaps it was the old boredom. Once the novelty wore off and he'd settled into a routine of meals and days at sea, something in him would have said, *All right, what's next?*

The first mutiny occurred aboard the *Saladin*. The crew, stirred to revolt by a man named Fielding, killed Captain Kenzie and his mate, broke into the booze, ran aground, and descended into a bacchanal on the shores of Nova Scotia, where they were seen by passing fishermen. In the end, the mutineers were arrested. A few were hung, including Fielding, but the rest, Hicks among them, were released. Hicks watched the men hang—the details would stay with him—then went back to sea. It was that mutiny, with Fielding teaching by example, that seemingly gave Hicks his basic template and educated him in the art of piracy.

He commenced his life's work soon after. According to the confession, it happened on a luckless whaler in the South Seas, where Hicks, in the way of Fielding, made the case to every man before the mast. *Do the figuring. What's zero profit divided by sixty? Zero. We could actually end up owing this sonofabitch money for expenses!* Among Hicks's gifts was a talent for persuasion. He quickly convinced a balance of the crew that it was their right to get into the rum and have a party. He led the assault on the officers: knocked 'em down, locked 'em up, went on a bender. In the end, once they'd sobered up and understood their situation—no one knew how to properly set a course—they surrendered. As the captain could not punish all the mutineers—without a crew, he too was lost—he punished only those who were considered instigators. Possibly for no reason other than that he was young and handsome, Hicks was not suspected. The "ringleaders" were locked below, where they spent the rest of the voyage in irons. As soon as the whaler reached port, they were carried off the ship half dead and locked in a local jail.

Hicks quickly mastered the art of revolt, establishing a wildly effective pattern. He'd join a crew, labor till bored, then begin working on the other sailors, paying special attention to the angry and outcast. He'd stoke their resentment till it was red hot, then use a random incident to touch off a melee, kill the officers, get into the booze, and flee with the money. At some point, he killed his first man. He'd previously come close, in the woods during his prison escape. He knew he could do it if he had to. Then he had to. He actually came to enjoy it. Some men acquire the taste.

Hicks found a partner along the way. They became a dreaded team, legendary like Butch and Sundance, had Butch and Sundance been less charming and more violent. But who knows? Maybe Butch Cassidy was not so different from Albert Hicks. Hicks's partner first appears in the confession as "a steerer"—a helmsman on a whaler. From his place at the tiller, he kept an eye on young Albert Hicks. When Hicks touched off a mutiny, the steerer joined in, then followed Hicks into town, then to the next ship. He's eventually given a name—Tom Stone. Hicks did not mention that name until hours into his confession, then in a strangely matter-of-fact way. "Tom Stone . . . that was his name. . . . I do not think I've mentioned it before."

Was Tom Stone a real name or an alias? It's too common to be traced, so it was probably fake. It was not the name that mattered anyway; it was the relationship. These two men traveled and robbed and killed together for years—slept side by side beneath the stars on the decks of ships; camped in the fire warmth at western outposts; lived in the same houses and hotels, stormed cities, busted up casinos, and shared secrets. Not much is known about Tom Stone: Was he sloppy and mean, or precise like a harpooner? Was he blond and wild, or soft-spoken and dark? We know only that, for over a decade, he and Hicks were inseparable.

In the whaling trade, all routes led to the South Pacific, with its archipelagos and atolls, its island kingdoms. Hicks and Stone turned up there in the 1840s, when large parts of the region were still unfrequented by Westerners and seemed as mysterious as lands in fairy tales. They arrived on a whaler that had not had much success—the crew was thirsty, looking for action. Once the ship anchored in the palm-fringed bay of what seemed a deserted island, fifteen sailors, Hicks and Stone among them, were sent ashore in two yawls to gather food and water. They beached the boats and scattered. A few climbed the palm trees to shake free some coconuts. Others went into the forest to gather figs. Such uncharted islands had a wild smell that put northerners in a bewildering trance. The sound of waves, the rattle of fronds . . . *There will be no consequences. You have returned to an earlier state of creation.* They hacked open the fruit with machetes, then drank the milk. As they were loading the yawls, strange men emerged from behind the trees—Hicks called them "natives." They were in a state of undress, carrying spears. There was a standoff, then a hand-to-hand fight, the men so close each could feel the other's breath. Hicks brought his machete into play. In a moment, several "natives" lay in the sand. The rest retreated. This battle pulled a lever in his mind, Hicks said. It gave rise to bloodlust, an urge to kill again. He told the men on the beach it was time. *We'll return to the ship, attack the officers, lock them in the hold, and sail to America.*

The men seemed to agree, then got back into the two yawls. As they crossed the bay, Hicks said, "As soon as we're on board, select [a] man, kill him at once."

Hicks tried to keep up with the other yawl, but it zipped ahead. The men from that yawl were climbing onto the whaler before Hicks was across the bay. If he expected to see a flash of blades or other signs of mutiny, he was disappointed. The sailors in the first yawl sounded the alarm and reported on Hicks and Stone, who, as soon as they got up the rope and over the gunwale, were beset. The mutineers fought back but were bloodied and subdued and locked in what Hicks called "double irons," their hands and feet bound in shackles like those he'd wear in the courtroom in Manhattan. A week later he was on deck when the ship sailed into a beautiful port that Hicks called Wahoo in what Captain Cook had dubbed the Sandwich Islands. Wahoo was in fact Oahu, the volcanic island where most Hawaiians still live.

Hawaii was still autonomous in the 1840s and '50s, an antipodean paradise governed by an ancient royal family. The water around it was filled with longboats and surfboards. The waves that would become legendary curled as they broke offshore. The wharves were crowded with every kind of ship from every place on the planet.

Hicks and Stone were neither reported nor arrested. Who had time? They were given one last thrashing, then set free. Honolulu was the big town on the island, a post-card picture of red roofs and steep green hills. Captain Cook had been the first European to visit the island—that was in 1778, just sixty-five years before. Modern technology had followed, then disease. The population was halved by smallpox, yet the place remained a kind of nirvana, God painting with a different set of colors. Pine-apples were piled on market tables beside sugarcane and molasses. Hicks and Stone wandered the streets wide-eyed, amazed.

What happens when you set the devil down in paradise?

The pirates hung around the waterfront saloons, gathering information about the island. They stole money and rented a house in the hills. In the distance, they could see Mount Ka'ala, the highest peak on Oahu. A small white house with a tin roof became their base of operations. They'd lay up all morning, then set out at night, down into the dark alleys and ginger-choked squares. They went on what Hicks called a "spree," an orgy of stealing and boozing satisfaction. "For a long time we led the life of freebooters, robbing and plundering wherever we went, and dissipating the proceeds of our robberies in the wildest debauchery."

The pirates eventually aroused suspicion. They were stopped and questioned. No one knew what they had done, but they were rough-looking foreigners with no apparent means of support. *Lock 'em up.* They were detained in a dank prison, each morning the same. Gruel, the chattering voices of drunks, the harbor pitifully blue beyond the prison bars. In the end, they were saved by a sea captain. Several members of his crew had jumped—a common occurrence in Hawaii. He needed men, so he came to the jail and asked if there were any sailors among the inmates. Hicks and Stone went directly from their prison cell to another whaler.

A few weeks later, anchored off the coast of an island a thousand miles from Honolulu, they jumped ship, fleeing with guns and knives. Hicks identified the place as "Typie Bay." It must have been Tahiti, French Polynesia. They should have vanished into the jungle, set up in a thatch hut, married beautiful local women, lived a thousand months as if they were a single day, stood on the cliffs watching the sun sink into the firmament. They should have welcomed Typie as a chance for a new life. Hicks should have relaxed and changed. But he was a predator, a wolf, "the worst man who ever lived." Such a person does not change, not even in paradise. He and Stone were caught breaking into a house. Just like that, they were back in jail.

It was a Dutch captain who sprang them this time, the commander of a whaler registered in Amsterdam as the *Villa de Poel.* The ship was bound for Magdalena Bay, across the Pacific in Baja California. Magdalena was a mecca for whalers. They came from around the world to hunt the grays that mated there each winter.

Crossing the Pacific Ocean took forever, it seemed to Hicks. He worked up a burning hatred in these weeks, the kind of hatred that, on other occasions, would've had him reaching for an ax. But the entire crew was Dutch. He and Stone could barely communicate with them, let alone stir rebellion. He fumed instead, vowing to take off as soon as they reached Magdalena Bay.

Whalers were scattered across the waters when they arrived. Hicks and Stone could hear men everywhere, talking and laughing. The pirates got into a yawl and hit the water with a crash. They started rowing. The shore was a tangle of moss vines, a mangrove swamp. Once on land, they hiked till they reached a town. Mexico before the American War was a desolate land of stone churches and cobblestone squares, as sleepy as the Spain of Cervantes. Hicks and Stone, perfectly at ease, set off on an epic crime spree. It would've been hard to tell them from the western bandits of lore. Yankees on horseback, they drank in cantinas, raised hell in villages, slept it off on a beach or in a hammock that swayed in the breeze. Hicks was thirty-one, thirty-two, at the peak of his power, broad-shouldered, clear-eyed, and handsome. His hands, weathered and large, folded across his stomach as he dozed.

Whenever word got out that a sheriff was looking for them, or whenever they got bored, they'd switch from land to sea, or vice versa: 1851, 1852—Hicks blurred the years into a run of cities and towns, Cabo San Lucas, Valparaiso, Mazatlán, spinning past like numbers on a

roulette wheel. They encountered stevedores and merchants, import agents, an immigrant banana man sepa-
rating ripes from turnings on a broken-down dock.
Booming American industry was already endangering
their wanton way of life. It would soon become impossible—no wild places left, no pirate islands. But for years
they stayed a step ahead of the law, always coming or
going, dropping or raising anchor, taking a berth or stealing away, counting the money, torching the ship.

Deputy Marshal De Angelis, while hearing the confession, tried to keep track but soon lost count. Just how
many men had Albert Hicks killed? Was it twenty?
Thirty? Fifty?

Hicks said he was not sure himself.

Who was this man Hicks? the police wanted to know.
Was he really a pirate? That was how the newspapers
described him—Hicksy, the last of the old buccaneers,
the last Blackbeard, the last Calico Jack. But we think of
pirates working together in a bandit crew, operating in a
hierarchy, following a constitution, pledged beneath the
Jolly Roger. Hicks was different. He called himself a free-
booter. He went about his work piecemeal, either alone
or with a single partner. He did not attack frontally in the
way of the famous pirates, but infiltrated, subverted, and
overthrew. He was more like a virus, a dissident from a
gangster nation, a shadow republic that exists all over the
world. He was a perfect example of a pirate who adapted
to the modern age.

"After a lapse of a few years, during which time I
passed through a series of adventures too numerous to
mention, and the details of which would fill a volume"—
gambling dives, whiskey and women, a succession of

towns—"we found ourselves in Lower California about the commencement of the Mexican War," Hicks told De Angelis.

Hicks and Stone wanted to get as far as possible from the fighting—if you were not careful, you could end up in the goddamn army!—so they took jobs on a U.S. store-ship that was headed up the coast to Santa Cruz Bay, California. They had no intention of staying on this ship—they were merely catching a ride. Soldiers patrolled the decks, making it a tricky jump. They waited for a moonless night, then stood on deck at two or three in the morning. The coast boomed past, unwinding like a rib-bon. They stashed guns and other supplies in a yawl—it hung over the water on chains—then climbed in.

Hicks looked to the left, then to the right. He and Stone seemed to be the only people awake in the world. To make certain, he dropped his hat into the sea. Was it a Monmouth, a wool cap that sailors wore to protect them-selves from the salt and the sun in the 1800s? Or was it the Kossuth hat, with its wide brim? Gripping the side of the yawl, he watched the hat drift down and disappear. It must have hit the water, but no one, it seemed, was around to notice. So Hicks released the yawl, which dropped with a clatter of chains, metal on metal. The fall seemed endless, like plunging into a hole, deep and dark, or going through the mouth of a whiskey bottle into another life.

Hicks and Stone hit the water. Teeth rattled against teeth. Shouts came from the deck. The pirates scrambled for the oars and began to row. There was a short burst of fire, then a fusillade. Guns from another ship were shoot-ing at them as well. Bullets peppered the water—it was grapeshot—getting closer and closer, as if seeking out the yawl. They found it, as Hicks and Stone were pulling up onto the beach—it was cut to pieces beneath them.

The forest began fifty yards from the shore. They ran for it, drawing fire as they went. They got into the trees, dense and overwhelming sequoias. "We remained in this wood for a few days, and then travelling on, we reached the city at night, where we stole horses and made for the mines," Hicks told the deputy marshal. In need of cash, they robbed travelers on the road, prospectors leading pack mules a-jangle with pickaxes and shovels.

On January 24, 1848, gold had been discovered in Sutter's Mill, a shithole of a factory town in northern California. The mineral shone through the wild river, amber and black. Word reached Hawaii before it reached Boston. The *New York Herald* carried the story on August 19, 1848: THERE'S GOLD IN THEM THAR HILLS! Hundreds of thousands of men were soon on the move, the so-called 49ers, in carts filled with shovels and Bibles, with the worn faces of prospectors, down-and-outers with mad vacant stares—if you leaned close, you could see their pupils looked like dollar signs. They traveled by road and sea or signed on to whalers, only to jump ship in San Francisco.

These men, all in search of a claim—it was the American dream in its purest form, wealth for the taking, neither work nor virtue necessary—hiked into the wilderness that started beyond town. Some dug, while others panned the cold, clear rivers. At night, a hot wind blew through the mountain passes. Bare slopes and flawless skies—California was still as the conquistadors had seen it, mules humping across the soft brown swells that led to the Pacific.

The country was awash in optimists intending to strike it rich. *Gold fever!* Stick a pan in a stream, and bang! You were eating a filet on Geary Street. Hicks and Stone had got the news along with everyone else. While most people were searching for a vein, the pirates were doing a much easier sort of mining—finding people who'd already found gold, then taking it away. For six months, they tramped through the hills, menacing the camps, most of which consisted of three or four men—a tent, tools, an accumulating pile of dust, the product of six or seven months of labor. The camps were isolated, a half-day ride from help, protected by an idiot with a rifle. There were no cops, no soldiers. The land was lawless—no order other than what you imposed. It was an ideal setup for desperadoes, a buffet, a smorgasbord. They could go in, take what they wanted, then head back for more.

Hicks and Stone worked at night. They'd infiltrate, rob, and kill—"dead men tell no tales." They believed many of their deeds were mistakenly credited to Joaquín Murrieta, a Mexican bandit who'd became a populist hero in gold country, robbing the rich, killing the arrogant, hounding the Yankees. Murrieta was said to be the real-life model for Zorro. "I have no doubt that, during this period, many of the crimes attributed to the notorious Joaquín were committed by us," Hicks said. "The devil, whose work we were so industriously doing, seemed to protect us."

Having accumulated a fortune—Hicks said they had more gold than they could carry with both hands—the pirates decided to blow it all in San Francisco. What if you did whatever you wanted, as much as you wanted, every way you wanted? How long would it take you to spend it all?

San Francisco was a boomtown in 1855—not so different than Cuzco, Peru, in 1550 or Leadville, Colorado, in 1882. In a heartbeat, it had gone from nothing to everything, from a small Spanish mission and fort called Yerba Buena to a wild metropolis annexed by the United States and renamed for its picturesque bay. Between 1846 and 1850, 200 inhabitants became 21,000. It was less a city than a stampede, a delirium. It can feel like that still, cresting and falling on great floods of commerce: beat poets, hippies, computer programmers. It's insubstantial as a result, pumped up, phony. From a distance, it's a picture on a soap bubble—towers, bridges, sea. You hold your breath, waiting for it to pop. When Hicks and Stone arrived, it was ramshackle, with houses of redwood and pine, the smell of sawdust, the ring of hammers, storefronts packed onto the hills. Certain landmarks were already in place—the Presidio, the Spanish Mission, the nonsensically pitched streets that climb to heaven, then plunge to earth. Mansions and silversmiths, bordellos, the harbor, smoky islands that dream of China.

Hicks rented a hotel room near the wharf. Dropping a sack of gold onto the desk, he said, "Tell me when I've gone through that." Stone installed himself on the same floor, blinds drawn against morning light, chatter of seagulls—the Pacific Ocean means the end of America. The city had grown so fast, people were living in tents, in driftwood shacks. There were dozens of high-end clip joints, ten percent houses, wolf traps. Every bar was a casino, offering a million ways for you to lose everything you'd dug out of the hills. Faro was the preferred game, but aficionados had begun to branch into poker and draw. The sound of cards being shuffled, the clatter of dice, the dealers—this fantasy California existed, if it existed at all, for only a moment. On certain nights, Hicks knew he was "the mightiest man in the world." "The barroom, the brothel, and the monte table, were the only attractions for us," he explained. "For six months we led the life of demons, leaving no bad impulse, no fiendish purpose, no gross passion, nor any wicked design, ungratified and unaccomplished."

And then he ran out of money. It was gone. He'd found the bottom of the bucket, gambled, boozed, and whored it all away. So . . . back to the till . . . back to the machine . . . back to the water.

The fate of the *Josephine,* a brig that shipped from the foot of California Street, San Francisco, was like a premonition of the fate of the *E. A. Johnson.* The ship was bound for Valparaiso, Chile. Having heard its holds were packed with silver doubloons, Hicks and Stone signed on as hands. They performed diligently while awaiting their moment. It came a few miles off Mazatlán, Mexico. As the crew—four or five men—slept, the pirates armed themselves, went down to the cabin, and subdued, tied, and bound everyone. They crowded them into a yawl and set it adrift. In control of the brig now, they methodically gathered every bit of the treasure—more money than they'd started with in San Francisco, more money than they'd ever seen. They set fire to the *Josephine*—it burned off the coast at dawn—climbed with their loot into the other yawl, dropped into the sea, and headed for shore. As they approached Mazatlán, it grew larger and filled with detail, dusty streets and rickety houses, rocky hills.

There were ancient chapels in Mazatlán, Spanish churches, and cliffside houses that kept vigil over sun-baked market squares.

They had to do something with all that cash—a hundred thousand gold and silver doubloons, the equivalent of millions today. It was more than they could carry or store, bury or explain. They had to launder it, though that's not the term they used. They came up with a solution that would not be unfamiliar to a modern-day drug lord: they bought a hotel and a bowling alley in Mazatlán. The first indoor bowling alley had opened in New York a half decade earlier. The sport, if it is a sport, had become a sensation. The pirates lived in the hotel, a seedy wreck not far from the beach that catered to a rough crowd. Many of its guests were fortune hunters, prospectors heading to or from the mines.

Hicks developed a routine: sleep late, have coffee in the bar, talk to guests, perhaps ask one of them—a Mexican businessman reading *El Boletin,* say—what was happening in the world. In 1853 Franklin Pierce was in the White House, and the Rangers killed that Mexican Robin Hood, Joaquín Murrieta, in California. Then he would head out. Hicks walked every inch of Mazatlán. He was thirty-three, a big gringo, as handsome as a stage star. He dressed like a sailor waiting for a ship, in canvas pants, a striped shirt, a knee-length peacoat (the sort known as a monkey coat), and a broad-brimmed hat. He wore a ruby pinky ring and took snuff. He was not a dandy, but did know how to dress. He'd switch clothes after sundown, head back to the bar, and spend the evenings drinking with guests. He was always gathering information. Where had this man arrived from, and where was he going? Was he born wealthy, or had he recently come into a fortune? Whether rich or poor, flush or busted, Hicks continued to rob and brutalize—because that's who he was and that's what he did. He paid special attention to well-dressed travelers, examining their companions and horses. If the setup looked good, he'd rouse Stone, and they'd follow the traveler after he checked out. They'd strike beyond town, at a quiet place along the road, emerging from the shadows, hats pulled low, Hicks waving a silver Colt pistol, the so-called Navy Revolver. *Give us what you've got. The coins, the paper. All of it. Now.*

They were also willing to improvise. The world is various and vast; no one knows what the wind might carry. One evening they happened across a wagon train fronted and backed by men riding squat donkeys, the sort the Spanish call burros. It was on the road from the mines. Hicks and Stone killed the guards, then got into the saddlebags. They were amazed by what they found: dozens of freshly minted silver bars, each stamped with the name of its owner and the name of the Mexican state, SINALOA. They had to be worth at least $200,000, but how could you spend or trade them? It was like coming into possession of a famous work of stolen art—both invaluable and without value. They were too heavy to carry—even a few bars would be a burden. They took a shovel from one of the donkeys and dug, burying the treasure a few hundred yards off the road. Hicks offered to sell the bars to a Chinese trader for $25,000, a man Hicks called "the Chinaman, Cassa." Cassa agreed to ride out and take a look, but he refused to bring along the purchase price, fearing, as he told the men, that they'd simply shoot him and take the money. Hicks laughed: *You're right about that, amigo.*

They never did figure out what to do with the silver bars. They're probably out there still, buried beneath a shopping mall or highway.

Suspicion soon fell on the hotel. Misfortune had come to so many of its guests. Mexican authorities investigated. Getting word of it—it took only a few questions—Hicks and Stone packed their duffels and cleared out. They rode fifty miles inland to the old town of Valparaiso, a colorful village in the hills that knew only two seasons: sunshine and rain. They'd gotten away with maybe fifty thousand dollars, part of which they used to buy a boardinghouse in the outskirts. They tried to continue as before, gathering information on miners and traders, robbing them outside town, but Valparaiso was smaller than Mazatlán, and word spread fast. They escaped a step ahead of an angry mob and raced back to the coast, a fortune in their saddlebags.

Mexico was finished for them—they'd become too well known, burned clean through it. They caught a ship, made a stop in Peru, then sailed through the strait and on to Rio de Janeiro, Brazil, an ancient city for this part of the world. Rio's foundations had been laid in 1565, but the old Portuguese town had been remade by waves of Dutch, French, English, and Chinese immigration. With its horse-drawn trams and cobblestone plazas, its huge varied population, Rio was as modern as any place in the world in the 1850s—it was coffee shops and theaters, libraries, the opera, rich expats living beside the dirt-poor descendants of the city's first inhabitants, masters and slaves. Portuguese was the language, but a dozen other tongues could be heard in the markets—Spanish, French, Dutch, English, Chinese, and Ladino as well as fast-

disappearing Amazonian tongues. The most prominent
citizens owned rubber, sugar, cotton, and brazilwood
plantations in the provinces.

Hicks and Stone rented a house near the harbor and
spent most of their time in the groggeries that lined the
docks, tough cavelike joints that served beer, Canary
wine, and a Portuguese drink called Ginjinha. Days went

by, a phantasmagoria of boozing and gambling and sleeping it off. So it continued, on and on, from drunk to sober, from affluent to busted, from sated to hungry. There were hardly more than two successive hours in which Hicks was not inebriated, his handsome face gone sloppy and slack, stupid smile and pinprick eyes, drinks for everyone. He remembered Rio as a "debauch"—liquor and women, flashing knives, cards, cotton skirts spinning across ballroom floors, slaves in clanking chains, gauchos driving herds through the side streets, peasants in tall hats—afternoons and nights, laughter and brawls and a single slug left in a bottle when the sun appeared above Guanabara Bay.

After they'd gone through the last of the cash, they sobered up, bathed, and went back on the road, a Latin American road this time, headed south. They followed the old highway—now walking, now riding—from Rio all the way to Montevideo, the capital of Uruguay, fifteen hundred miles down the coast. It took them through faded port towns: Santos. Paranaguá. Punta del Diablo. Punta del Este. They robbed and killed along the way. "There is many a whitened skeleton bleaching by that roadside now, on the same spot where it fell by my murderous hand, and the traveler, as he rides along, will see many a place where the grass grows taller and greener than that which surrounds it but little dreams that its roots are enriched by blood shed by me," Hicks told Deputy Marshal De Angelis.

On the road, Hicks and Stone hijacked a party, a man and three women—they were clearly aristocrats, members of society who'd made the mistake of going riding in a wild, unsettled country. Their beautiful white horses suggested breeding. The man wore a fine suit, and the women wore jewels. Hicks described this incident at length in his confession; it was one of the few times he showed mercy. He seemed to consider it a turning point. Once you see your victims as people, you're finished.

In the confession, Hicks spoke of his intent to rape the women—it's the ony time he talked like this. The pirates separated the man from the women, knocked the man to his knees, then went through their bags and pockets, taking anything that looked valuable. "We robbed them and should have killed them all, but the women were beautiful, and, for once, I allowed my heart to yield to the soft feeling of pity," Hicks said.

> "I shall never forget the look of these poor frightened creatures kneeling at my feet, praying to me to be merciful, while my partner, Tom Stone, stood a few feet off, with his [gun] at the head of the man who was gradually divesting himself of everything valuable he had about him. One of the women wore half-a-dozen magnificent diamond rings, and the other carried two gold watches set with diamonds, besides other trinkets of great value. These I made them take off, and give to me. After which, I intended to have ravished and then killed them; I halooed to Tom to get rid of the man, and come and toss for the choice of the women—but the younger of the two, though I spoke in English, seemed to be aware, as if by instinct, of our designs. She started suddenly up, and, with a bound, sprang to the side of her husband, and clung to him in such a way that Tom could not kill him

without killing her also. I seized the other woman, and was about to execute my hellish purpose upon her, when, with tears and prayers, she besought my pity, and begged for mercy. . . . I do not know how it was, but my heart softened for once, and I stopped Tom's hand just as he was going to pull the trigger on the man, who now stood alone, with his arms folded, awaiting his fate. Tom looked astonished, but put up his pistol with an oath, and after some demurrer, agreed with me to let them all depart without further harm. I even assisted them to catch their horses, which they mounted, and rode back with all the speed they could toward Montevideo. Ten minutes after they had gone I felt sorry, and thought I had acted like a fool."

The pirates soon accumulated a new fortune, which got them to Argentina. They posed as businessmen in Buenos Aires, which, like Manhattan, was set in an estuary, a swell of land on the western shore of the Rio de la Plata. By 1850 the city was a capital in the European style, an outpost on the edge of the pampa.

Hicks and Stone lived there quietly, letting the days wash over. For a beat, it seemed they might continue like that forever. No running or being chased, no blood or confusion, just the ordinary pleasures of ordinary life. They had the money for it but, as it turned out, not the temperament. Two months of humdrum had them itching for action, which they figured they'd find back in the United States. They took jobs on "the bark *Anada*," a three-masted ship with rectangular sails bound for New Orleans. They could have gone as passengers, but they did not want to lose control of their luggage, with thousands of dollars sewn into the linings. They worked before the mast instead.

The voyage started without incident. Then as the *Anada* was sailing through the West Indies, with a lush island in the distance—a beach and a mountain, a peak in the clouds—the cabin boy, who was very young, ran afoul of the captain. There was a scuffle. The captain decided the cabin boy should be punished in the open before the crew and the passengers. He stripped the boy to his knickers and tied him to the mast. The captain took off his coat and uncoiled the whip. He stood ten feet from the boy, talking as he drew back. While the crowd watched, the captain snapped his arm, delivering the first blow. The whip cracked before it touched skin—that meant the tip had accelerated past the speed of sound. Each stroke left a stripe on the boy's back.

Hicks told De Angelis of the pitiful cries—that kind of suffering, on that particular day, was too much to take. Maybe he saw himself in the boy. Maybe he saw himself as he'd been before Norwich prison. He pushed through the crowd, knife in one hand, a spike in the other. He cut down the boy, who fell whimpering to the deck. The captain grabbed Hicks, who quickly dropped him with the spike. Members of the crew set upon Hicks, who fought them off with knife and spike, joined by Tom Stone. Between them, the two took control of the *Anada*. They locked the passengers in a stateroom, tied up the crew, robbed the ship, loaded the loot into a yawl, plunged into the sea, and headed for the island, which turned out to be Barbados.

They soon found work on an English brig bound for

New Orleans, but some of the crew must have heard about the *Anada* mutiny because, soon after the brig was under sail, people began to glare at Hicks and Stone. Conferring together, they decided to flee before they could be caught. Near the mouth of the Mississippi River, they took off in a dinghy. They rowed into the bayou, into murky water as thick as stew, between the shacks and the gators, between swamp islands that vanished at high tide. They wandered until they found a road.

New Orleans was already fading by the time Hicks and Stone turned up, an elegant place that had been allowed to dilapidate. Once America's great southern port, a transit point for every bit of grain grown west of the Allegheny Mountains, its decline began soon after the first railroad was built. It would eventually degrade from commercial dynamo to museum of past glories. In the 1850s the city was filled with sailors, river men who floated down the spine of the nation on rafts and side-wheel steamers. The big ships stood in a tremendous armada at the edge of the French Quarter, sending up columns of black smoke that turned to ribbons in the subtropical sky. The city had been French, then Spanish, then American, then French—an effect of the migration that followed the Haitian slave revolt, which, in the 1790s, filled the streets and markets with exotic food and brass bands. In the 1800s New Orleans minted coins in both English and French. On the back of the ten-cent piece was the word DICE. Sailors used the term to identify the city. Dice became Dixie, which came to characterize the entire region.

New Orleans entered the Union as part of the Louisiana Purchase. It was a focal point in the War of 1812. In the Battle of New Orleans, fought after the war itself had ended—as usual, the city was late—General Andrew Jackson joined with the pirate Jean Lafitte to beat back the British. In other words, New Orleans was kind of a pirate city. The island-filled bayous that lurked beyond the outskirts, a region created by the Mississippi Delta, had long been a hideout for buccaneers.

Hicks and Stone took rooms in the French Quarter, which filled the river bend that gave the town one of its nicknames: Crescent City. The streets are confused as a result of the geography. You never know exactly where you are in New Orleans, only that it's too far and too deep. The air smelled of resin, bananas, coconuts, ale, tar, wood, tobacco, burning fields, horseshit, sweat, and industry. The docks were ramshackle: weeds came through the paving stones where society ladies stood before grand store windows. The wooden sidewalks were made from rafts that had come down the river. Royal, Chartres, Esplanade—the streets were lined with brightly colored houses, red and pink, absinthe green, curaçao blue, fronted by French balconies with iron facades. The stalls of the French Market glistened in a warm rain. The Mississippi looked like café au lait. The square at the center of town had been renamed for General Jackson in 1815. The taverns were boisterous: in the Napoleon House at 500 Chartres, a room had been set aside for the deposed dictator should he make it off Helena. At Lafitte's Blacksmith Shop, at 941 Bourbon, the pirate had once fenced stolen goods.

Hicks and Stone drank and slept till boredom overcame them. It was not money they craved but excitement. They studied notices posted beside the piers, then signed on to a ship bound for Liverpool, on the west coast of England. A capital of the industrial revolution, it was powered by textiles. Cotton was a crucial ingredient in that revolution, and much of it was shipped from New Orleans. The boom enriched planters and mill owners, sea captains, investors, and insurance men on both sides of the Atlantic. That explains the lucrative circuit Hicks and Stone traced in the 1850s, a triangular route of villainy that followed the cotton trade. They'd sail from New Orleans to Liverpool, then from Liverpool to Rio, then from Rio back to New Orleans, robbing at every opportunity. They'd hit ships and traders, fat cats and sailors, then return to their starting point and go again.

The life of a nineteenth-century sailor was boredom shot through with incident. Even the dull hours were shadowed by the expectation of danger. The more time you spent on the water, the greater the certainty that tragedy would befall you. For many, Albert Hicks and Tom Stone were that tragedy, but of course, the pirates themselves were not immune. For them, disaster often came in the form of weather, a cyclone, a monsoon. A few miles off Waterford, England, a tremendous gale caught their ship, the *Columbus,* commanded by a Captain McSerin. For a moment, the ship stood atop a monstrous roller— from there you could see the entire topography of the storm, black clouds illuminated by lightning—then skimmed the face and was dashed to pieces. A moment later Hicks and Stone were in the water, clinging to wreckage as the *Columbus* slipped beneath the waves. Most of the crew died, but the devil drifted the outlaws till they could be rescued. They'd lost their treasure, saving only what they had in their pockets.

They spent two or three days drying out, then went back to work—Liverpool, Rio, New Orleans—until they were again overcome by weather. It happened in America this time, a dozen miles from the Alabama coast. Hicks described the location as "Off Blackwater Banks." A huge storm, a hurricane cooked in the warm waters of the Gulf, hit their ship—the *Mobile*—like a broad flat hand. "The waves ran mountains high," Hicks said in his confession, "the wind blew great guns; sail after sail was carried away." The men wept and prayed, but it didn't help. Hicks put the total number aboard, crew and passengers, at eight hundred. In his telling, everyone died, "all but me and the devil."

"During the dreadful panic, I felt no fear," he went on. "I felt as if I was protected by a superior power, and only thought of how I could turn the loss of the ship to account."

He drifted for two days, lashed to "a spar, [before] I was picked up by a pilot-boat and taken into port, as the American Consul at that time will certify."

Tom Stone was among the dead—he had been Sundance to Hicks's Butch, the only man Hicks had ever trusted. The pirate took a moment in his confession—but no more than a moment—to eulogize his lost brother, "a brave fellow with a ready wit and a strong arm, ever on hand for any enterprise, no matter how desperate; and wicked as he was, I believe he loved and would have died for me."

Hicks was alone, as he'd been at the start. Solitude had its advantages. You had no one to share or disagree with, and no one to slow you down. Hicks caught a ship in Alabama—the *Jeanette,* bound for New York. There he caught another ship—the *Eliza,* bound for Boston. He met a new partner on the *Eliza,* a man he identified only as Lockwood. Little is known of Lockwood, not how he looked or spoke or where he came from, just that here was another marauding drifter who wandered the sea in a lawless age. "He was a strong, wiry man full of determination, cruel and desperate in his disposition, and totally without fear," Hicks said. "I found he had led a life nearly similar to mine, and he thought no more of stealing a purse or cutting a throat than I."

They started right away, commandeering, robbing, and sinking the *Eliza* off Block Island. It must be down there still, a ruin in the ribbed sand. From there, they continued in the old pirate way, looting, burning, scuttling. In Chile, they signed on to the *Ann Mills,* named for a British pirate who had distinguished herself in a battle with the French in 1740. (There's a portrait of this lady buccaneer holding up the head of a decapitated seaman.) The *Ann Mills* was an honest-to-God pirate ship. It had no country—it might as well have sailed from the netherworld—and operated under a black flag.

Hicks told Deputy Marshal De Angelis that he finally found his element on the *Ann Mills,* a ship "where I could gratify the highest object of my wicked ambition. I was a free rover, with no one to fear, and no one to obey." He spent a year on the *Ann Mills,* sailing from Marseilles to the Dardanelles, from Constantinople to Gibraltar. Now and then the pirates smuggled alcohol. Now and then they smuggled slaves.

What did Hicks have inside? At times, it seemed like he had nothing inside, just appetite and anger, a simple drive to avenge whatever slight he believed he'd suffered.

At other times, as when he rescued the cabin boy from whipping, you sensed there was something, that his was a soul in torment, trapped and deformed, battling its own nature. Hicks personified a certain kind of struggle—in the violence he visited on the world, in the war he was waging, but also in that interior battle. His was a rotten body of which devils had taken possession, but better angels were there, too, buried beneath an accretion of harbors and days.

Following one big score, for reasons never properly explained, Hicks split with Lockwood. Sometimes you just want to go it alone. A handshake on a London dock, turn and face the wind. Hicks was fixed for money, ruddy and strong. His good looks were dangerous in that they set people at ease. Since his release from Norwich prison, almost two decades had passed in a blaze of mutiny and murder. He planned to return to New York. He was getting old. A pirate at forty is like another man at seventy—he has lived so rough for so long and done so many terrible things. He has lost all faith in human nature, turned his back on God. He is the most cynical creature in the world.

Hicks hired on to a British steamer carrying emigrants from Ireland to the United States. Called the *Isaac Wright,* it was no different from a dozen other brigs that took devastated multitudes across the Atlantic—one hundred thousand Irish made the crossing in 1847 alone. The ships left from Dublin, Limerick, Belfast, Londonderry, and Galway, bound for New Orleans, Baltimore, Boston, Philadelphia, and New York. It was a hard crossing, days and days on a rough sea, disease spreading from passenger to passenger. As many as 30 percent of Irish emigrants died in 1847. Some called the ships floating coffins. Healthy passengers, fleeing the cramped cabins, slept on deck. You've seen the pictures: all those faces, women in black as if dressed for a funeral, men in snap-brim hats, moth-eaten coats hanging from their emaciated frames. In the background, the Emerald Isle fades away. In the distance, America.

Hicks spotted a young woman on the *Isaac Wright*. She was with her family. He spoke to her on deck, then took extra care of her for the rest of the voyage. He found her again in Manhattan, took her on walks, then visited when her family moved to Albany. He presented himself to her parents as a hardworking, God-fearing Christian man, but they didn't believe it. He was unsettling—that sudden flash of anger, those hands.

They married anyway, then moved to Connecticut, then kept on moving. They settled in New York City. Hicks tried to live like other people, but he returned to crime whenever he needed money. When he should have been at home, he walked the docks, listening to the waterfront gossip, forever searching for a certain kind of ship. "I kept a sharp lookout for small craft bound for cargoes of fruit, oysters, and in a quiet way gathered all the information I could in regard to the number of hands they shipped, and the amount of money they generally carried."

He looked for a ship with cash and a small crew— low-hanging fruit. *Just once more, to set up me and the missus.* He found the perfect target in the *E. A. Johnson.*

The sloop went to sea on March 20, 1860. Hicks waited till the captain and one of the hands was asleep below, took an ax off the pilothouse wall, and stashed it at his side. The older Watts brother was at the helm, "and I asked him to allow me to steer a little while," Hicks told Deputy Marshal De Angelis. "He consented and went forward. In a few minutes, I left the helm, and, taking the ax, went to him and asked him if he saw Barnegat Light. He said he did not. I told him to look again, and pointed with my hand. He turned round and looked in my face a moment, but even if he had suspected my cruel purpose, he could have read no indication of it there, for I was calm as though I were going to do the simplest and most innocent thing in my life.

"Look again," said Hicks. "I'm fairly certain that's Barnegat Light.

"He turned his head, and peered through the darkness in the direction I pointed, and as he did so, I struck him on the back of the head with the ax, and knocked him down.

"Thinking I had not killed him, I struck him again with the ax as he lay upon the deck."

Hicks killed Smith Watts next—"the edge [of the ax] crunched through his neck, severing his head from his body"—dealt with Captain Burr, then finished off Oliver Watts, who'd survived the first blows.

"My bloody work was done," he told the deputy marshal. "Dead men tell no tales.

"My intention was to run the sloop up the North River, then fire her," he continued, "but I came near running her on the Dog Beacon, abreast of Coney Island and Staten Island lighthouse, after which I fouled with a schooner, and carried away the bowsprit, so I put the money and other such articles of value as I could pick up, into the yawl, and then sculled ashore three miles, landing just below the fort on Staten Island.

"My movements after landing are well known," said Hicks, "and when I look back upon the fatality that seemed to dog my steps, it seems as though the fiend who so long had stood by me in every emergency had deserted me at last, and had left me to my own weakness. But I never thought of this until after my arrest. I had no shadow of a presentiment that I should be checked so suddenly and brought to justice, and on my return to New York, made arrangement to go away with my family as coolly as if nothing had occurred which should counsel me to use caution."

Hicks had reached the end of his confession. The deputy sat quietly, swollen in the way of a dishrag, having soaked up all that blood and grime. "I ask no sympathy, and expect none," Hicks said at last. "I shall go to the gallows cursed by all who know the causes which will bring me there, and my only hope is that God will, in his infinite mercy, grant me that spirit of true repentance which may lead to pardon and forgiveness in the world to come."

Did Marshal Rynders believe Albert Hicks's confession? How about Detective Nevins and P. T. Barnum? It would be published on the day of the execution, then reported and quoted by newspapers across America, so editors were satisfied it was true, happy to profit from the ambiguity, or accepted it as a kind of folktale. It's possible that Hicks made up the story to get money for his soon-to-be widow and soon-to-be fatherless child. It's possible he made it up to please his audience—everyone plays the room. It's even possible that the writer tasked with turning the notes into a narrative stretched some of the details supplied by Hicks. But there's good reason to believe the confession was largely true. When published, lawmen from around the country used it to solve several unsolved crimes, closing the book on robberies and murders. But in the end, maybe it doesn't matter that much. This was the story told by the pirate—that's what counts. It tells us either about his deeds and adventures or about his inner life and sense of self. It's a dreamscape. Even if you doubt the words, you can still be terrified by the music.

News of Hicks's confession, that outlandish rambling life, murder and piracy on the seven seas, quickly spread. If he had been famous before, he now became something more—a dark star, a symbol of all that was twisted in this raw country. He was the soul of America, courageous yet grotesque. The nation had begun with certain ideals, but reality was different. On our money, in our public places, we have images of the founding fathers, but there is another set of founders—underworld kingpins, gang lords who slept late, never went to an office, never answered to a boss. In Hicks, the public caught the image of such a man at cask strength. He spent his entire life outside the law, living by his own rules, following a creed that is the American creed stripped of all decency and sophistication. Albert Hicks personified this nation no less than Andrew Jackson, who drove the Cherokee down a trail of tears. He was the violence used to build the great cities and conquer the West. He became an antihero partly because people ignored his actual crimes and partly because he seemed to demonstrate reality instead of lie—he did whatever he wanted and took as much as he could, just like Cornelius Vanderbilt and Jay Gould. He was the masses in the shape of a monster—the best at being the worst. We need Al Capone and John Dillinger and Albert Hicks if only to show us that someone is living in defiance—absolute criminality is absolute freedom.

The more people knew about Albert Hicks, the less they seemed to understand. Questions filled the penny press: *Where did he come from? What is he actually like? Is he truly different, or is he one of us? How did he get this way?* Was his fate inevitable, cooked in him from birth by biology or God? Was he born evil? Or had there once been hope—could things have turned out differently?

When these questions became overwhelming, the authorities contacted Lorenzo Fowler, New York's famous phrenologist: he could read your personality in the shape of your skull. He could answer every question, solve every mystery.

By 1860 Lorenzo Fowler and disciples had turned phrenology into a rage. Fowler had learned about the science, or pseudoscience, in his second year at Amherst College, in 1831. In a lecture, the visiting German philosopher Johann Spurzheim said phrenology had been pioneered in the late 1700s by Josef Gall, an Austrian physician who believed the nature of a person's character could be read in that person's skull. A phrenologist is a "doctor" who feels your head, mapping every bump and abnormality the way an astronomer maps mountains on the moon. Each place in your skull, as shown on the porcelain phrenology models that still crowd curio shops, was associated with a particular trait. A swelling in a certain spot would manifest in an excess of a certain trait. These traits were so eccentrically named and defined— see *Phrenology: A Practical Guide to Your Head* by Lorenzo N. Fowler—that people were convinced the science just had to be true: conjugality (monogamy, union for life, pairing instinct); philoprogenitiveness (parental love; attachment to one's offspring; love of children, pets, and animals, especially young or small); alimentiveness (appetite, feeding instinct); ideality (perception and admiration of the beautiful and perfect). A big head meant you were probably selfish; a bump in back of the head, opposite the eyes, meant you were probably the sort of person who would stick with a task—killing every single

person on an oyster sloop, say—until that task was accomplished. As a general rule, good people had symmetrical skulls with wide-set eyes, while lunatics, maniacs, and hatchet wielders had lemon-shaped heads, dead eyes, and weak chins. In short, a person's fate was prefigured in the shape of his or her skull.

Fowler fell for phrenology for the reason confused people tend to fall for ideas that make too much sense. It explained everything. No more mystery or confusion. No more sin or redemption. No more free will or guilt. Who could be condemned for committing even the worst crime if it was preordained in the frontal lobe?

Lorenzo Fowler, sharing a byline with his brother Orson, published the definitive text, *Phrenology Proved, Illustrated and Applied,* in 1836. It went through at least sixty editions—it was the best seller that mainstreamed the movement. He trained Orson in phrenology, and together they opened an office at 135 Nassau Street in Manhattan, charging one dollar for a basic reading, and three dollars for a deep analysis, walk-ins welcome! In the early 1840s, with business booming, they moved to 308 Broadway, a short walk from the photographic studio of Mathew Brady. Many famous Americans visited both shops the same day. Taken together—daguerreotype, phrenological study—you had the entire person, outside and inside. Horace Greeley, Ralph Waldo Emerson, and Margaret Fuller all sat for Fowler. The abolitionist John Brown was examined a few years before his raid on Harpers Ferry. According to the report, Brown had "firmness and energy enough to swim up the Niagara River and tow a seventy-four-gun ship, holding the towline in his teeth." General George Custer, on the other hand, was diagnosed as the type "inclined to overdo." Walt Whitman included his phrenological report in the first printing of *Leaves of Grass*.

Albert Hicks, a few days before his execution, was escorted in shackles to Fowler's Broadway office. The shingle in front said FOWLER AND WELL'S PHRENOLOGICAL CABINET. As his skull was examined, perhaps Hicks closed his eyes and thought of the sea, or the heft of a knife, or the roughness of a hawser, or the cry of the albatross, or the echo of a foghorn in the muddy streets of lower Manhattan, a shofar calling the sinners to the Temple to repent, or Charlie Parker blowing his alto sax in the dream future of the same town.

Hicks was unusual. Based on his crimes, you'd guess him to possess an idiot's skull, undersize and studded with protrusions, as misshapen as a busted watermelon. He in fact had a beautiful cranium—not the skull of a philanthropist or a concert pianist, maybe, but not that of a killer, either. "He has a remarkably strong muscular organization and bony system," according to Fowler's report, "which has a powerful influence on the tone, quality and direction of his mind. His mental temperament is fairly developed, but not to such an extent as to give the finer qualities to the mind and character. He is excitable, and susceptible of intense feeling, yet it is rather a heated impulse of passion, than a delicate and refined sensibility."

Of course, if you took your time and really knew your business and examined closely, you would find the abnormalities from which tragedy followed as sure as the night follows the day. Fowler made special note of the area associated with combativeness—above the right ear—which was "strongly developed," exaggerated in a way that suggested "a power to overcome obstacles, and if provoked, and had some selfish purpose to subserve, render him capable of almost any act of desperation." Hicks's alimentiveness was equally overdeveloped, proof that he was the sort that "loves to gratify the appetite highly, and is liable to indulge it too freely." But the key flaw was not excess but lack. A flat place above the eyes—an area associated with spirituality—resulted in the outlaw's failure to believe in or heed the metaphysical. "His Spirituality is deficient," Fowler explained. "He has very little idea of the unseen, and of subjects pertaining to the higher life, and has scarcely any Veneration at all, which leads him to act without due regard to the Higher Power, and without feeling his dependence on, or much responsibility to, his Creator."

Phrenology succeeded, for a time, because it expressed a universal fear—that we are not in control of our own fate or even our own actions, that we are playthings of biological forces that can neither be seen nor escaped. Deficiencies in our nature, flaws in our makeup, bumps in our skull—that's the entire story. We call phrenology a pseudoscience because it turned out to be incredibly wrong, even ludicrous, but it did get at a greater truth, which is why Lorenzo Fowler was such a hit in antebellum America. He came not as a charlatan but as a precursor and a premonition of Darwin and Freud and abstract expressionism and punk rock and free-form jazz and dada and existentialism and nonsense. It was not a working medicine he gave us but a picture of the world controlled by invisible forces. It was a world we can almost understand but never control. It was a world at night, sketchy and filled with shadows. A great force was at work in this world, but it was not God, and it did not care about us. It was the same force that had made Albert Hicks and sent him out to sea. It was Albert Hicks.

Fowler ended his report with a thought that would become typical of the coming century: it was not the man who had failed the system, but the system that had failed the man. Hicks might have been good, but the decrepit towns and institutions, life on the wheel, had made him bad. "The crimes that he has been led to commit are full as much the result of a want of the right kind of education, as from his natural organization," wrote Fowler. "He has strong passions, and an unbending and headstrong will; but with proper culture and good circumstances, he would most likely have used his energy and talents in a way to secure success and respectability, instead of warring upon the right and interest of his fellow men."

In other words, though we cannot take Fowler's report on Hicks seriously, though every sentence in it is antiquated and silly, it nails a deeper truth as sure as Captain Ahab nailed the doubloon to the mast of the *Pequod*. Hicks was the sum of his flaws—almost good, which, in practice, is the same as evil. In the end, his only hope was to be loved and cared for by parents and prisons and institutions, but that was not the American way, and the result was this monster, those severed fingers, that ghost ship. Fowler included a line in his report that captured the terror of the coming age: "If you are not with God, then everything is permitted."

———

P. T. Barnum sent his plaster of Paris expert to see Hicks in the Tombs. He sat close to the killer, preparing the concoction, chatting as Hicks breathed through a tube and the cement was applied. The result was a death mask made from a living man. Such a mask reveals the features as if for the first time—nose and eyes, forehead, cheekbones and jaw all so close together—look how small the real estate a human face actually occupies! Beethoven, Napoleon, Disraeli, James Dean, Robert E. Lee. You get the same sense from every famous death mask.

Is that all there is?

When the plaster was removed, Hicks would have seen himself as a fossil, as if spied from the future. It was the face that would outlive him. The mold was carried back to Barnum's American Museum at Ann Street, where, in a few days, it would be filled with wax. When the wax cooled and the plaster was stripped away, you would have Albert Hicks all over again. Then the body would be built—it would be shown in action, wielding an ax. It would be better, Barnum told Hicks, if the clothes worn by the figure were genuine. Barnum proposed a trade: new store-bought clothes for the rags Hicks had on his back. Prison clothes were not issued until after sentencing, and in the case of Hicks, who would never make it to prison, they would not be issued at all. If not in court, he'd be wearing the same clothes in which he'd been arrested—pants, shirt, jacket. He happily made the trade with Barnum, believing he—Hicks—had got the better of the deal. He soon changed his mind. *Just look at this shoddy stitching,* he complained, *how the coat comes apart at the seams—how it itches!* His own clothes had been of a higher quality. Hicks had an innate sense of style—see the monkey coat and the Kossuth hat, see the silk shirts picked up everywhere from New Orleans to Buenos Aires.

Barnum would have his Hicks on display within a week of the execution. The figure would be exhibited alongside Ned the Learned Seal and Crowley the Man Horse. The placard beneath it read: "Life-Size Wax Figure of A.W. Hicks, attired in the very clothes worn by him when he butchered his victims with an ax. Acknowledged by all to be a wonderful likeness of the infamous pirate!"

THE EXECUTION

Albert Hicks turned talkative near the end. He spoke to reporters and politicians, to dignitaries, to anyone who would listen. He would scratch the rash left by his carny clothes and run a finger through his beard. His grin was terrifying. You never knew what such a man found funny. He struck up a friendship with the kid in the next cell, Mortimer Shay, who was at the center of his own infamous trial. Just twenty-one, Shay had killed a man named John Leary at Crown's Corner, a grogshop in the Five Points. Shay had joined in a fight involving a friend, hitting the friend's attacker with the blunt end of a knife. He believed he had done the right thing—protecting a friend—but now was no longer certain. He had not expected the man to die. Hicks had followed the case closely. In some of the things he said to Shay—the imminence of his own death gave Hicks freedom to speak plainly—you glimpse a code: *You saved your friend. There can be no wrong in that.*

One afternoon Hicks sent word that he wanted to talk to the press. A few reporters were always hanging around the Tombs. When these men gathered outside Cell 8, Hicks told them he'd composed a song and wanted to perform it. He'd committed the verses to memory and sang in a high, wavering voice:

> *My own, my dear loved mother!*
> *If I could see thy face,*
> *I'd kiss thy lips in tenderness,*
> *And take my last embrace.*
> *I'd bathe thee in my awful grief,*
> *Before my fatal hour,*
> *I'd then submit myself to God—*
> *His holy will and power.*
> *Near the town of Foster,*
> *Is the place where I was born,*
> *But here in New-York City*
> *I'll end my days in scorn.*
> *I shipped on board the* Saladin,
> *As you may understand,*
> *Bound to South America,*
> *Captain Kenzie in command.*
> *We arrived in that country*
> *Without undue delay,*
> *When Fielding came on board,*
> *Ah! cursed be that day!*
> *He first persuaded us*
> *To do that horrid crime*

We could then have prevented it,
If we'd begun in time.
I stained my hands in human blood,
Which I do not deny.
I shed the blood of innocence,
For which I have to die.
They led them up the plank,
Unto the fatal stand,
And there they viewed the ocean
Also the pleasant land.
A cord adjusted through the ring
Then stopped their mortal breath;
Forthwith the whole were launched
Into the jaws of death.

The meaning of the first lines seems clear—they follow the pirate's biography. It was the second half that confused reporters. It was about a hanging that seemed to come as a punishment for a terrible crime committed aboard a mysterious ship, the *Saladin*. None of them knew the story. Was it an actual crime or a figment of a condemned man's imagination?

Soon after the poem was published, though, letters began arriving from Nova Scotia that confirmed the truth of the lyric. According to the *Times*,

> the mysterious allusions by [Hicks] to his agency in
> the piracy and murders on board of the *Saladin* . . .
> have led to a discovery of all the facts concerning
> those events, which have been volunteered by sev-
> eral persons who were cognizant of the circum-

stances of the case, and who have called at our office, or sent us communications on the subject. . . . Among these is a gentleman who was a magistrate of the County of Guysboro, Nova Scotia, in the year 1844, and who was one of the persons who boarded the wreck of the *Saladin,* as she lay bilged among the rocks, some twenty-five miles east of Halifax, her piratical crew being at the time carousing on shore with their ill-gotten plunder. He states that, as near as he can recollect, the vessel was run on shore in a clear day in the month of June; that the crew had thrown overboard [the] Capt. . . . After sinking all the boats but one, by loading them with copper bars, they escaped to the shore, carrying with them some $80,000, mostly in Mexican silver, which had been divided amongst themselves, and which they had in bags, kegs, &c. It was two or three days before anybody, except the fishermen, had any knowledge of the wreck, and it was wholly owing to the extraordinary conduct of the pirates on shore that they came to be suspected, and were finally arrested and conveyed to Halifax for trial. On boarding the bark, her decks, cabin and railings presented every appearance of a recent and sanguinary struggle. Everything was in disorder; fragments of clothing and other articles bestrewed the decks, indicating that the crew had plundered the cargo before taking to the boats. A Government vessel carried the crew to Halifax, where they were arraigned, convicted, and several of them hung.

As this account suggests, nineteenth-century pirate culture in North America was less like that depicted by Robert Louis Stevenson than like the rough-and-ready society described by Hunter S. Thompson in *Hell's Angels* or by Nicholas Pileggi in *Wise Guy*. We tend to set pirates behind a kind of veil, in a fantastic past. We separate old-time American pirates from the modern variety working off the Horn of Africa, say. The world inhabited by Albert Hicks in Rhode Island, New Orleans, and New York seems as unreal as a costume drama—villains out of *Peter Pan*, in puffy shirts, who, at any moment, might break into song. In truth, the life led by Hicks and his cohorts was more like that led by modern gangsters and outlaw bikers—the conveyance and the road were different, but the marauding spirit was the same. It was a life of hardship and danger, thrill and escape. They lived that way because they were sick and demented but also because they could not stand to live any other way. Only they knew pure freedom, the pleasure of utterly sating the basest appetite.

You sense the pleasures of pirate life in the fate of the *Saladin*. Hicks would have been around twenty-four at the time, not long out of Norwich prison, still new to the wild world of portside taverns and open sea. In his depiction of the mutiny, you recognize the joy of the young gangster blazing through his first days, before the sin accumulated and the whole thing turned to ash. It was about overcoming the captain and getting into the booze, drinking till the mermaids surfaced on the wine-dark sea. It's telling that, in his last hours, when he should've been getting right with God, Hicks was singing not about heaven and hell but about an early act of infamy. In the end, his mind returned to the beginning and to the crime that started the years-long spree.

The date and place of execution had been set by Judge Smalley: Friday, July 13, 1860, Bedloe's Island. Some say it was this hanging, New York City's last public execution, that forever cursed "Friday the 13th."

The day before, Isaiah Rynders went out to take a look at the island, which is really just a big rock between the Upper and Lower bays. Named for its first European owner, Dutch merchant Isaac Bedloe, the island had been the site of several earlier pirate hangings. It was one of those haunted places where pirates lived and died. (Part of Captain Kidd's treasure is said to be buried on Bedloe's, though no one has ever found it.) Rynders walked the perimeter, chose the best spot for an execution, then oversaw the construction of the gallows, which he'd carried on the cutter.

This particular scaffold had been in use at the Tombs for over a dozen years. According to a press account:

> It consists of two upright posts supported by timbers, into which they are framed and braced at the bottom, and surmounted by the cross-beam at the top. The condemned person is stationed immediately beneath, and at the given signal is lifted suddenly from the ground, by the fall of heavy weights, to a height of several feet. If the cord has not been carefully adjusted with due regard to the compression and rupture of the spinal cord, death takes place by the tedious process of suffocation, the

person often apparently conscious for many minutes.

Rynders chose a gentle hill a few dozen yards from
the beach on the east side of the island. From there, the
condemned would be able to see the entire theater of his
monstrosity: Manhattan, New Jersey, Brooklyn, and the
harbor. The fact that this same island, under a new name,
has for decades been the home of the Statue of Liberty,
needs no additional comment.

By the end of the day, the marshal was back at his
desk, greeting a stream of visitors who'd come for tickets
to the hanging. He traded some, sold others, and gifted a
few to patrons.

July 12, 1860. The last morning, the last afternoon, and
the last night. Long shadows fell over Manhattan. Number eight, like all cells on the Murderers' Corridor, was
without windows or vents. Hicks's final hours were given
over to prison sounds and prison smells, a narrow barred
view, a slice of corridor, visitors going past. It's an oddity
of perception: the less you are shown, the more you see
and hear. In the distance, so far off that it fades to white,
is the hum of the city, horses and wheels, the cacophony
of the market, the world as it will be after you are gone.

Hicks was somber at the end. Thinking and praying,
eyes like saucers, he hardly ate. He was an ascetic. His
focus was on the next life. His wife, who had been angry,
seemed either to forgive or simply to forget. He was her
only friend, the father of her child, the author of her
problems, her great love. She was allowed to sit with him

inside the cell. They huddled together whispering. Some of their exchanges were overheard and reported. They spoke about the future—she had one, he did not. They spoke about money and the child. She would get cash from the confession, which would be published the next morning. Some believed Hicks had hidden additional money, a pirate treasure. He seemed to hint at it. Asked about the situation of his wife, he told a policeman not to worry, that she would be "all snug."

At five-thirty P.M. Father Duranquet arrived. The final hours, the crisis in the shadow of the rope—this was the priest's specialty. He was a kind of escort. He led you to the threshold of the next world. He nodded at Mrs. Hicks, then told her it was time to leave. The cell was filled with people: the priest, deputy marshals, prison officials. It did not allow for intimate last words between husband and wife. There was no crying or cursing. Hicks gave her two small books—one was a Bible—took her hand, looked her in the face, and said, "Goodbye."

Then again: "Goodbye."

She said, "Goodbye, Willie. Willie, goodbye," turned and left.

Unescorted, without baby or other family, she went into the street and was quickly swallowed up by the city.

Hicks spent the rest of the evening with the priest. He asked questions, and Father Duranquet answered honestly. There are some things we know but many more that we do not. He read from Scripture. He was like a holy man in an old movie, long and lean, with thick veiny hands and a pocked face.

Hicks's last meal was brought in at eleven P.M., though no one called it that or made it any kind of big deal. No filet, no lobster, just tea and "light refreshment." He ate and drank, then got onto his straw mattress. It amazed people how calmly he did all this on what had to be the most terrifying night of his life. According to the police, he lay down at midnight and within five minutes fell into "a sleep so sound that even the entrance of the keepers during the night did not wake him."

The moon rose and fell. The wind blew from the West, where Simon Hicks was raising a glass to a luckless brother. The stars turned around the sky. A guard woke Hicks at four A.M. Asked how he felt, the prisoner said he "never slept better in all [my] life." The priest came in when Hicks was dressed. They prayed together. The deputy marshals, those who had experience with condemned men, were waiting for him to fall apart, but it did not happen. "When engaged in prayer with Father Duranquet, his face bore a meek and sorrowful expression," one said later, "but as soon as the religious ceremonies were concluded his countenance resumed its natural expression of firm indifference."

The warden came to say goodbye. "Hicks shook him warmly by the hand," according to an account, "thanking him for the many acts of kindness he had received at his hands, bade him a last farewell. The culprit then remained closeted with his father confessor for an hour or so, and declined seeing any person other than his spiritual adviser."

Marshal Rynders appeared in the doorway at nine A.M., in dress uniform. He told Hicks the task he now had to perform was unpleasant. Hicks said he knew it and also knew the marshal was only doing his job. Rynders took a document from his pocket and read it out loud. It was the death warrant. That finished, the marshal told the prisoner to prepare himself to die.

Hicks dressed in an outfit made specially for the occasion—tailored and paid for with the help of the Freemasons. In the next world, the currently condemned would be king. It was electric blue, as gaudy as any suit worn on Broadway. "His coat was rather fancy, being ornamented with two rows of gilt navy buttons and a couple of anchors in needlework," according to a report. "A white shirt, a pair of blue pants, a pair of light pumps, and the old Kossuth hat he wore when arrested, completed the attire. Hicks was exceedingly cool while engaged in arraying himself in his fancy suit, and seemed as unconcerned about his approaching doom as though the idea of death had never crossed his mind."

Hicks walked along the Murderers' Corridor, saying goodbye to fellow inmates, chatting with the guards. He thanked them all, lingering before the cell of his neighbor Mortimer Shay. Hicks then went through the big doors and out into the sunlight.

A huge crowd had gathered on Franklin Street to get a last look at the pirate. Some called out, others cursed, admonished, or jeered, but most merely stared. Hicks was more than just a criminal and more than just a killer. He was famous, a celebrity, a star. Fliers had been glued to brick walls up and down the Bowery. They advertised the execution as you might advertise a traveling carnival: *Cruise to Bedloe's Island, enjoy beer and all you can eat oysters while watching the hanging of the notorious Pirate Hicks. One Dollar.*

Newspapers were stacked along the curbs. Hicks could not read, but he would have recognized his name. All carried reports on the confession. The document itself was for sale at kiosks, bound between covers, fronted by a garish headline.

THE CONFESSION OF ALBERT W. HICKS

Pirate and Murderer

ASTOUNDING CONFESSION AND

STARTLING DEVELOPMENTS

MADE BY HICKS, THE PIRATE.

Ready THIS DAY (Friday, the 13th), The Day of Execution.

The Life, Trial, and Confession of Albert W. Hicks, the Pirate who committed the Triple Murders on Board the Oyster Sloop Edwin A. Johnson, in New York Harbor! This most startling confession was made by him to the US authorities, and the proceeds of its publication guaranteed for the benefit of Hicks's family, this being the only consideration upon which he would reveal a Tale of Crime which identifies him with the commission of NEARLY ONE HUNDRED MURDERS!

Hicks talked to George Nevins and Elias Smith—the detective and the reporter—outside the Tombs. They'd only played their part, but being responsible for the death of another man is a hell of a thing. Hicks greeted them like old friends.

Smith said he was sorry.

"No hard feelings," said Hicks.

"How do you feel about the future?" asked Smith.

Hicks pointed to Father Duranquet, saying, "That is a matter I would rather leave to him." He thought a moment, then added, "I am resigned. I will not say anything on the island."

"I forgive you," Hicks told Detective Nevins.

"I'm glad to hear it," said the detective.

Hicks climbed into a closed carriage, seated between Marshal Rynders and Father Duranquet. The driver cracked the whip, the horses moved, the wheels turned, the houses and buildings of lower Manhattan moved backward outside the coach windows. The driver turned east onto Canal, a dramatic change from the chaos in front of the jail. The streets were empty, the avenues deserted. Even then New York had the almost magical ability to absorb any sort of event, no matter how lurid. Go a block, turn a corner, and it's gone. As Hicks had only a few hours left on earth, you imagine him trying to experience each moment—value comes from scarcity—the shadows and the colors, the brick buildings, the smell of horses, the smell of summer.

It was a ten-minute ride to the harbor docks. The carriage slowed as it reached the pier where the ship that would carry Hicks to Bedloe's Island was waiting, a side-wheel steamer called the *Red Jacket*, a ferry chartered for the occasion. It was bedlam on board: hundreds of people, many of whom had been drinking for hours, awaited the pirate. There were twice as many on the wharf. It was like a painting by Bruegel: stevedores and seafaring men, fixers and gangsters, all pressed together, shouting and laughing. "The police [experienced] considerable difficulty in keeping the crowd back," the *Times* reported. "By strenuous exertions a passage was finally obtained,

and Capt. Rynders ordered the carriage in which the prisoner was to drive on to the dock. The eager crowd, which
had already got access to the pier, now besieged the carriage, and literally broke in the windows and tore away
the curtains to get a sight of him. The only notice which
he took of these proceedings was a derisive smile."

Hicks was led from the carriage and through the
crowd, shoved and taunted, the priest always beside him.
It was even worse on the ship. The saloon was open, and
vast quantities of what the newspapers called "lager-
bier" had already been served. The early hour meant no
breakfast, which meant people were drunker still. And it
was blazing hot. "The scene on the ship defies description," wrote a witness. "A crowd of some 1500 persons,
perhaps, had assembled onboard, and the most intense
excitement prevailed. Gamblers, fighting men, ward politicians, reformed drunkards, actors, medical men, city officials, and bogus reporters without number, formed the
great bulk of the motley crew."

Hicks was brought to what was normally the ladies'
salon. He sat on a couch and dropped his head in his
hands. "He seemed to be thinking," the *Post* reported.
He stood as the ship glided into the harbor estuary, he
walked across the cabin and looked out—the city, houses
and wharves, mansions and slums, were turning into distance. The crowd chanted and howled. They wanted to
see Hicks, but the prisoner refused to come out. He was
kneeling beside the priest. The deputy marshals had left
them—police guarded the doors. A reporter looking
through an interior window watched Hicks pray. This
was the only moment, according to the reporter, that the
condemned man showed the slightest emotion. His face

flushed, his brow furrowed. But when he stood, he was as impassive as before.

Hicks asked to speak to Marshal Rynders. The men stood side by side, talking in the heat of the day. Hicks again said he would make no statement on the island. There'd be no last words, no plea for forgiveness. Hicks said he wanted it done and done fast. In the meantime, he would talk to no one but the marshal and the priest.

Hicks went outside and stood at the rail. The *Red Jacket* followed the Manhattan shore. The prisoner was a dozen feet from the side-wheel, which churned the river into white water. The police kept the mob at a distance but could not stop people from gawking. Many were bothered by how calm Hicks appeared. They needed to see remorse in him—terror and tears. He "looked . . . on the river, evincing no show of feeling," the *Times* reported, "but for the fact that he was known to be the man who was to die, his apparent unconcern for the great event of the day, would not have struck anybody, as he would simply have been set down as one of the crowd of spectators. As it was, known as he was, as Hicks, the pirate, whose moments of life were ebbing with every revolution of the paddles that threw back the spray of the hissing water almost in his face—those who saw him wondered, and came, perhaps, reluctantly to the conclusion that the man had no human feeling. Probably those who said so did him wrong, but his coolness and self-possession were at least remarkable, even for a great and hardened criminal."

As you approach the end, everything becomes a clock—the sun as it crosses the sky; the coast as it slides past; the side-wheel as it turns. Time ebbed from Hicks, as it does from everyone. That is what makes a character like the pirate so poignant and pathetic. In these moments, bad as he was, he stood for all of us getting closer to the abyss every minute of every day. He was living the nightmare each person lives, only in public, among thousands who wanted to see him hang.

The *Red Jacket* was supposed to turn south and cross the harbor, but Rynders realized he was ahead of schedule. There was still time—lots of time. He remembered that the *Great Eastern,* a British ironside—considered a wonder of the age, it was six times bigger than any other vessel on the sea—was docked at Hammond Street, about two miles up the North River. It was the ship's first visit to the western hemisphere; it had been launched just over twelve months before. People were paying a dollar just to walk its massive deck. *Why not go see it for ourselves?* Rynders said to the captain of the *Red Jacket.* A moment later the steamer was heading north.

"After leaving the wharf the *Red Jacket* went to Bedloe's Island direct, most people would suppose," a *Post* reporter commented. "By no means. She took a pleasure trip up the river, to give those on board a chance to see the *Great Eastern.* We believe Hicks himself did not go to the windows to witness the mammoth steamer, but almost everyone else on the *Red Jacket* did. This, it must be confessed, is not a usual episode on the route to an execution."

They approached the ironside from the south, the massive ship rising before them. The passengers of the

Red Jacket, excited in the way of a drunken crowd, rushed the rail, nearly capsizing the steamer. Deputy marshals raced across the deck, screaming at the crew to redistribute the passengers. The *Red Jacket* cruised all around the *Great Eastern*—a seven-hundred-foot-long passenger ship with six masts, five funnels, two paddle bills, and a four-blade screw propeller—then headed back downriver.

The mob was laughing and singing. It was less a funeral procession than a Mardi Gras parade. Along the way, they spotted another remarkable ship, a brand-new U.S. revenue cutter, a kind of Coast Guard boat called the *Harriet Lane.* Named for the niece of President James Buchanan, it would prove to be even more interesting than the *Great Eastern,* for whereas the *Great Eastern* was huge, the *Harriet Lane* would have a life as unexpectedly storied as that of Albert Hicks. A few months after being seen from the *Red Jacket,* the *Harriet Lane* was drafted by the navy for use in the Civil War. Refitted as a gunship, it saw action at Fort Sumter, New Orleans, and Galveston, was captured by the Confederates, recaptured by the Union, then declared unfit. It was abandoned at sea in 1881. It caught fire and burned for days.

The *Red Jacket* reached Bedloe's Island just before eleven A.M.—a tremendous moss-covered rock, green and gold, the scaffold visible, the rope swinging. The Upper Bay was crowded with ships full of spectators who wanted to see the execution. "Steamboats, barges, oyster sloops, yachts and row boats," according to a report. "They had come from all parts. From Connecticut, where the murdered captain and the brothers Watts belonged; from Long Island, where they were well known. Large steamers, such as carry hundreds of people away on pleasure excursions were there, so laden with a living freight of curious people, that it seemed almost a wonder they did not sink incontinently. There were barges with awnings spread under which those who were thirsty imbibed lager-bier. There were row-boats with ladies—no, with females of some sort, in them, shielding their complexion from the sun with their parasols."

"Public executions are almost always regarded by a certain class as festival occasions, somewhat less expensive and vastly more entertaining to behold than a circus, or rat-bout by terriers," the *Post* reported, "but seldom, in this city at least, has an execution been turned into a great gala festival. . . . At Bedloe's Island thousands of people came to witness the execution; eleven steamboats and a vast fleet of sailing vessels and skiffs accommodating the immense crowd, among which were a number of females, who came down as on a picnic to witness the death struggles of an atrocious villain. A party of fancy men"—sports and dandies in woolen tailcoats with brass buckles and buckskin pantaloons, carrying gold-knobbed walking sticks and jewel-studded snuffboxes—"on their way to meet and welcome the [bare-knuckle] prize-fighter [John C.] Heenan, stopped for a few minutes to look at the execution."

It was as if everyone Hicks had ever known or hated or been hated by turned up for the final scene of the violent play—to watch him hang until they could be certain he was dead. "Prize-fighters, shoulder-biters, keepers of low-drinking saloons and persons of a similar class" is how one reporter described the crowd. "On the trip they ate, drank, and made merry. It was a very delightful excursion, undoubtedly, this sailing down the bay, at the expense of the city, to see the death of a bloody pirate—altogether quite an amusing and pleasant way of spending a bright July morning."

There were nearly as many people on the island itself. They'd been drinking and were drinking still. They met the *Red Jacket* with a tremendous cheer, then rushed the landing, ready to lynch the killer before he could make it to the scaffold. Marshal Rynders stood on the pier, trying to quiet them, his voice sharp, rank with authority. He had participated in gunfights on the Mississippi River, been chased out of frontier towns, fought battles in the Five Points and in the city legislature. He commanded respect from the crowd, and the crowd did its best to give it, but the crowd was drunk. He had to hush and scold, scold and hush for several minutes. He called for order— *We have not come to celebrate,* he said, *but to see a man die.*

Meanwhile a navy ship had arrived from Fort Hamilton in Brooklyn with a detachment of marines—young and fresh-faced, as handsome as toy soldiers with rifles and bayonets. Marshal Rynders had arranged it, foreseeing the hysteria of the crowd and knowing he'd need more than a few dozen deputies to contain it. The use of federal troops to control a local population was not that unusual at the time. More than once in the 1800s, guardsmen had been sent to quell the rioting gangs of New York.

The marines pushed the crowd aside, then formed two lines, ten feet apart. The soldiers faced the crowd, creating an open space, a corridor that led uphill from the pier to the scaffold.

As in a wedding, Marshal Rynders carefully ordered the procession. Police and government officials exited the *Red Jacket* first. Then came those whom Rynders described as "real members of the actual press," as opposed to the hundreds who'd passed themselves off as reporters to get free passage to the island. Then came the physicians, who would make certain, when the time came, that the pirate was dead. Twenty of them had volunteered, simply to be part of the spectacle, but only three were tasked with doing the job: G. F. Woodward, A. C. Bell, and Guilmette Weltje. Then came the marshal with his deputies and lackeys. The pomp, the circumstance, the mayhem, and the spectacle—this must've been one of the great days of the captain's life. When everyone else was settled, Hicks made his way, with Father Duranquet on one side and a deputy sheriff on the other.

As the condemned man went up the hill, he would have seen a multitude of faces on land and at sea. Estimates put the crowd at twenty thousand. "A motley and strange scene indeed," according to a reporter. "On the water, there were not less than 10,000 to 11,000 present in costumes almost as variegated as at carnival. White shirts, red shirts, blue shirts, blue jackets, red jackets, green jackets, and every steamer, vessel and yacht, decorated with lively-colored flags, while the uproar was incessant—cries of 'Down in front,' 'Get out of the way'—rising from hundreds of throats at the same time."

The *E. A. Johnson* was among the ships. Selah Howell, its surviving owner, had had it fixed and painted for the occasion. Its name was written in big letters on the side. It was anchored beneath the gallows, between the scaffold and the city, where it could not be missed. A huge flag flown from its mast, described in the press as a "burgee," also showed the name of the ship. Howell said he hoped it would be the last thing the pirate ever looked at. Half a dozen people were on the *E. A. Johnson*, friends and relatives of the dead captain and crew. More relatives were scattered amid the crowd on Bedloe's Island. No one was there for Hicks. Not even his wife—she could not stand to watch, and it would not have been safe. She was to meet the body—when it was just a body—upon its return to Manhattan.

Hicks walked stiffly but steadily. He did not break character but remained stoic, expressionless. It's something witnesses remembered, along with his flashy blue suit and cold black eyes. It was the only freedom he had left—a refusal to show remorse, weep, or submit; a refusal to give the crowd what it wanted. He was living through this morning as he had lived through all the others—serene and detached, as if already looking back from the other side.

When he reached the top of the hill, he dropped to his knees and prayed for perhaps a minute, then stood and spoke his last words. Before he died, Lucky Luciano said, "Tell Georgie I want to get into the movies one way or another." Stonewall Jackson said, "Let us cross over the river and rest under the shade of the trees." Albert Hicks said, "Hang me quick—make haste."

The hangman stood by the scaffold. His name was Joe Atkinson, though everyone called him Little Joe. He'd been a carpenter in Brooklyn before he was recruited by George Isaacs, who served as city executioner until his death in 1852. George Isaacs, who'd been inspired by a book—*The Autobiography of Jack Ketch,* the "renowned high executioner of Great Britain"—trained Atkinson. ("I kind of eased into the business," Little Joe said. "I guess I just had a knack.") The press made a lot of the methods Little Joe learned from George—together, it was said, these men built a more humane gallows and made certain the procedure was not prolonged and no one suffered unduly, though at some level they must have just loved killing people.

George taught Little Joe how to run a memorable hanging—in addition to ending a life, an executioner should be a master of ceremonies. He oversees the erection of the gallows, the adjustment of the weights and ropes, but must also have a sense of showmanship. Little Joe would turn up on execution day with a flourish, like a director arriving at the theater on opening night.

Joe began his career with a double hanging on January 28, 1853—William Saul and Nicholas Howlett, the leaders of the Hook gang, who'd killed a night watchman on the schooner *William Watson* off James Slip—and continued until 1890, when he was replaced by the electric chair. In that time, he executed forty of the fifty prisoners put to death in the yard behind the Tombs, but considered the job he did on Hicks the highlight. It was the uniformed officials, the huge drunken crowd, the newspapermen, the nature of the criminal and his crimes, the snap of the canvas, the ladies with their parasols, the sailors in the rigging.

Little Joe was waiting for Hicks on the gallows. It was raised fifteen feet, reached by ladder. Joe carried a black hood in a silk case—a trademark. He slipped it over the pirate's head. For Hicks, there were just a few sensations left. The darkness inside the hood, the soft fabric, the scratchy rope as it was put around his neck. He stood there, the man in the sack, the pirate in the blue suit, the condemned man at the top of the world. The crowd became still. It made the kind of silence only a crowd can make. Ships jostled against each other in the harbor, toys in a bathtub. There was hardly any open water—just a carpet of vessels.

Marshal Rynders waved a handkerchief. The hangman pulled the lever, the weights dropped, and Albert Hicks was yanked with a release of kinetic energy high into the air. The noose closed, his head fell to the side. His neck had snapped at the third vertebra. It was 11:15 in the morning. His body danced at the end of the rope for three minutes, then was still. At 11:20, the body jerked once more—wildly—then was still in a different way. A few minutes later, the hands of the pirate and the neck below the hood turned purple. At 11:29, the body was lowered until the pirate's boots grazed the platform. The doctors came up—those three men. Each, in his turn, listened for a pulse and a heartbeat. One heard a murmur, a single contraction. The body was raised again, returned to its previous position as a half-cooked cake is returned to an oven. It was lowered at 11:45 A.M. and examined once more. This time, nothing. Death was pronounced. Then by way of thoroughness, and so the multitudes would have something to see as they sailed away, they raised Albert Hicks once more.

BURIAL AND RESURRECTION

Albert Hicks was cut down and placed in a coffin. "Upon removing the black cap which enveloped the head of the deceased, his features were found to be quite natural," according to a police report. "His face bore a calm expression, and nothing but a slight protrusion of the tongue denoted that death had been produced by any other than a natural cause."

The coffin was carried to a tug and brought back to Manhattan. By this time, the ships had cleared out, and the harbor had returned to its ho-hum quotidian weekday traffic.

The tugboat—*The Only Son*—delivered the coffin to the customhouse dock. Mrs. Hicks was supposed to meet the ship at the landing, but there had been a mix-up, and she was waiting on the wrong pier. By the time she figured it out, the coffin had been buried at Calvary Cemetery, a kind of potter's field.

Robbers dug up the grave soon afterward. When the police arrived, the coffin was empty, the body gone. It was likely sold to students at Columbia's College of Physicians and Surgeons, who were known to pay top dollar for fresh corpses, cadavers being in such short supply.

What happened to Mrs. Albert Hicks?

She would likely have moved into one of the poorhouses crowded on the waterfront alleys of the Fourth Ward, Dickensian structures buzzing with the desperate and destitute—there were dozens of these in the city before the Civil War. Or she might have found refuge in the big new almshouse that opened on Blackwell's Island (now Roosevelt Island) in 1845. It had a work farm where "vagrants" were taught "societal skills" and a nursery for children. It looked across the river at Manhattan, which might as well have been a light-year away. Or maybe, as her mother suggested, she found a place among the Shakers, a Christian community and Quaker offshoot named for the way its adherents trembled during prayer. The Shakers offered a home to anyone willing to believe, though theirs was a hard, celibate, strippeddown way of life. Or she could have left the boy at one of the city orphanages—a Catholic orphanage or a public refuge. New York's first such house had opened in 1806 on Raisin Street, with half a dozen children. By the time Hicks went on trial, most local orphans were being kept in a new brick structure at the corner of 73rd Street and Riverside Drive. Living in New York, this cruel city of winners and losers, of the fabulously rich and the pitifully poor, Mrs. Hicks and her son, had they drifted to the bottom, would at least have had company. There were twenty thousand homeless children in New York in the mid-1800s.

Or maybe she successfully fended for herself. By 1860, 15 percent of the city's workforce was female—nurses and seamstresses, punch press and sewing machine operators. Factory owners were especially keen to hire women, as they came cheap. Office work, maid or hotel work, a face amid a sea of faces, part of a great industrious army. She would have lived to see miracles, technological wonders—the telephone, the electric light, the Woolworth Building illuminated like a star in heaven—but remained a product of the city of migrant ships and waterfront dives. Or maybe she started over, left her son and went out west—"adopt your child and live out" is how her mother put it—another life in another town, Pittsburgh or Chicago, met, married, and loved again, a second child who never learned of the first. Maybe, years hence, she sat at the head of a Thanksgiving table, surrounded by grandchildren and great-grandchildren who knew nothing of the pirate in their family tree.

And what about her son?

Given a normal American life span, he would have lived through the Civil War and been in his prime at the start of World War I. Given a remarkable but not-unheard-of life span, he could have seen the Second World War, Elvis, and the birth of rock 'n' roll—just another old man, riding the IRT beneath the East River.

Detective Nevins went on to have a long and distinguished career. Elias Smith became a great reporter during the Civil War. Marshal Rynders lost power, overtaken by ignominy and scandal. He collapsed on a New York street in 1885. Apoplexy. He could not speak and went unrecognized for hours. He died that night. In a sense, all of these stories are really just a way of telling the story of the city. It boomed after the death of Albert Hicks, was torn down and rebuilt again and again, always different but always the same.

Today the Cherry Street crimp where Hicks had or had not been shanghaied, as well as the waterfront docks where he worked, are buried beneath the struts and pilings of East River Drive. Some of the tenements where Hicks slept still stand, though they've been turned from wino flops to hipster heavens. The Five Points neighborhood has long since been razed and built over—Paradise Square is now the site of Columbus Park, outside the federal courthouse. New York Harbor is the same, only not so wild—there are no pirates. Bedloe's Island is still there, only it's now called Liberty Island, home of the welcoming statue. Beneath the green lady, at her foundation, as her foundation, lingers the ghost of the dead buccaneer who, as much as any politician or tycoon, created the spirit and style and energy of the great metropolis.

Albert Hicks continued to dwell in Manhattan in the form of a wax figure until July 13, 1865, when, eerily, on the fifth anniversary of the hanging, P. T. Barnum's American Museum burned down. Imagine the man in the monkey coat and Kossuth hat succumbing to the flames, melting—first the nose, then the chin, then the coal-black eyes turning liquid and running like tears down the mottled face. He continued to exist in lore. His story runs like a ribbon through the history of the underworld. He was the bad man talked about by the gangsters who were talked about by the gangsters who were talked about by the gangsters I interviewed just yesterday. His story is there even if you don't know it. It's the iron and nickel beneath the molten liquid, beneath the magma, beneath the bedrock that is the surface of the earth.

Hicks's story became mythology almost as soon as he died. Within weeks of his execution, a pop song was written about the killer. Released by the H. DeMartin Publishing Company, it was sold as sheet music and played in parlors and at cotillions. It's a kind of murder ballad, like the *narcocorridos* that Mexican crooners sing about the rise and fall of infamous drug lords. On the page, it's called "Hicks the Pirate, Air: The Rose Tree."

> *. . . Upon this oyster vessel,*
> *A pirate bold had found his way,*
> *With wicked heart this vassal*
> *The Captain and two boys did slay;*
> *He seized the gold and silver*
> *Which this poor captain had in store*
> *His watch and clothes did pilfer,*
> *While he lay struggling his gore.*
> *. . .*
> *But the eye that never slumbers,*
> *Did follow on the murderer's track;*
> *And the vigilance of numbers*
> *To justice brought the monster back.*
> *. . .*
> *Twixt heaven and earth suspended,*
> *On Bedloe's Island Hicks was hung,*
> *Some thousands there attended,*
> *To see the horrid murderer swung.*

Hicks appeared before his biggest audience on April 4, 1963, when he was featured in the fourth season of *The Twilight Zone,* in an episode called "The New Exhibit." Wax figures in a museum, slated to be torn down and replaced by a supermarket, come to life and go on a killing spree. Among the murderers are Jack the Ripper and Albert Hicks, who is depicted with terrific accuracy right down to the Kossuth hat, sea ax, and black eyes.

Why does this story resonate?

Because it's too great and grisly to be anything but true. Because it gives you a picture of the New York underworld in an earlier incarnation—it's like a baby picture, the same city stripped of its subways and steel. Because Albert Hicks was a key figure, transitional, hinge—he belongs with Captain Kidd *and* John Gotti, the last pirate, a representative criminal in a city that was all about the ocean, but also the first gangster, a model for Lansky and Gambino. Because he is, in some versions, the victim, the shanghaied sailor who refuses to take it. Because he is a living demonstration of the fact that when you get into a dustup on a New York street, you never really know who you're dealing with. Because he was the worst made manifest. Because he was the danger and excitement of the city in the shape of a human being. He was a citizen of a city that was disappearing. He was a killer but an adventurer too. He could not function in a town ruled by the scientific method of a modern police force, or the studied probing of newspapermen. He had to go the way of the Daybreak Boys and the Swamp Angels, clear out to make room for the modern town. That's what was executed on Bedloe's Island, the man but also the breed, the era, and the age. It was the cops and politicians, the bankers and socialites and tycoons who owned the future. Albert Hicks had only the past—he was New York as it used to be and could never be again, the wild seafaring town buried beneath the towers and highways.

ACKNOWLEDGMENTS

My father said a thing not very long ago. He was running down the Golden Rule: *Treat your neighbor as you'd treat yourself.* "I've heard it my whole life, and I think it's bullshit," he told me. "I don't like myself very much, so if I treat my neighbor as I treat myself, that neighbor's getting treated like crap." That said, I'd like to thank the following people for helping me research, correct, copy-edit, untangle, or otherwise improve this book: Matt Levin, who helped dig out the old news stories; Sharon and Bill Levin, who birthed and raised Matt Levin; Steven Cohen and Lisa Melmed, for instilling in me a great love for New York lore; Ian Frazier and Mark Singer for early reads; ditto Dana Brown, Julian Sancton, and Neal Edelstein. David Lipsky for yeoman's work—and an ocean of support. Julie Tate for the fact checking. My agent, Jennifer Rudolph Walsh, and my editor, Julie Grau, who is *mishpucha.* And my friends—all of them. Especially Jonathan Galassi, Mark Varouxakis, Jonathan Lethem, Graydon Carter, and Jonathan Newhouse. My mother, Ellen Eisenstadt Cohen, who died but is still here. When I think back on events that came after her death, I recall her presence vividly. Which is weird. Aaron, Nate, Micah, and EZ, who taught me that any collection of people becomes a gang. And mostly Jessica Medoff, who married me a long time ago. She read this book again and again and again. Without her input, it would not be. And my father, Herb Cohen, who told me old stories, encouraged me to treat every human interaction as a game, and that the key to life is to care, but not that much.

A NOTE ON
THE PHOTOGRAPHS

With a few exceptions, the photographs in this book do not portray the people or events described. They instead show cities, harbors, and sloops, the world as it existed in the age of Hicks. They are meant to conjure the mood of an older America, the country of my great-grandparents, which is preserved, when it is preserved at all, in silver prints, daguerreotypes, and dreams. Most of the photos, which I kept near me while writing this story, come courtesy of the Library of Congress. The first image in the book, the one of John Gotti and his crew in front of the Ravenite Social Club on Mulberry Street in the early 1990s—that's different. It was taken by my friend Sara Barret, who happened across the gangster as you might happen across the first robin of spring. She asked if she could take his picture—Gotti was famously wary of photographers. He said, "Why do you want to take my picture?" Her answer—"Because you're a celebrity"—

touched his vanity. He said, "Yes, but just one." Look at the photo again—seeing how the men around the boss are acting, especially the thick guy in the foreground, it might not surprise you to know that this is in fact the second picture Sara snapped of Gotti that morning.

A NOTE ON SOURCES

I came across the story of Albert Hicks while researching my book on Murder Inc., the Jewish mob of Brownsville, Brooklyn. It was in the pages of Herbert Asbury's *Gangs of New York,* which reads like a Norse saga, illuminating a lost and unbelievably harsh civilization. Hicks occupied a special place in that civilization. He was its prehistory, its forefather. He was one of the Nephilim that turn up in the oldest parts of the Bible, giant bastard offspring of fallen angels and mortal women who walked the earth in a time of chaos and disorder. He was New York as it had been and could never be again, the city depicted by Robert Louis Stevenson in *Kidnapped,* the wild place of gibbeting and pirate saloons and mickeys and planks that must be walked. Hicks, as he appeared in Asbury—dark-eyed and handsome, collar raised to hide his face—was confused in my mind with every adventure, ghost, and pirate story I'd ever read.

I began to search for him in old newspapers and books. His depiction was different in each telling. Here he was pure evil, unredeemed by even a spark of hope. There he was Robin Hood, taking back his freedom with a hatchet. If I read about him at night, his image would appear in my dreams, shadowy, spectral, doomed to wander. I never considered him without thinking of John Dillinger, Blackbeard, Pittsburgh Phil Strauss, and Cain, the first killer, who'd been sent into the wilderness bearing the mark that both ostracized and protected him. Cain built the first city, so he is the father of every urbanite. And who was Albert Hicks but Cain in another guise, in another way?

He appears at the beginning of Luc Sante's *Low Life*, depicted as Asbury and every writer who followed had depicted him: a gangster and a seafaring man, drugged, kidnapped, carried unconscious onto a sloop, where, upon waking at sea, he was told "work or swim." They called this a shanghai, and for generations, it was an essential part of the story. It seemed to explain and even justify the killings. But when I began to examine the facts, the shanghai story fell apart. I'm not exactly sure how it started. It first appeared in print in Asbury, then reappeared in a score of other crime books. Perhaps Asbury invented it, because he liked it better than the real story. His book, parts of which appeared in the *New Yorker* in 1927, reads less like traditional reporting than like folklore. Asbury was creating mythology for the New York underworld, writing creation stories for the Fourth Ward and the Five Points. Facts gave way to archetypes, symbols. But I don't think Asbury made it up. I think he heard it from gangsters and neighborhood people, who, in the way of a game of telephone, shaped the facts into a legend, building up the story over time. It was the work of the city's collective subconscious. Herbert Asbury was just the first person to write it down.

In putting together this book, I've tried to strip away the accretion and recover Albert Hicks as he actually was—a story more complex and more interesting and terrible than any fairy tale. Hunter, scavenger, and waterfront dweller, he was the chaos hidden behind the official history. Telling his story is telling the story of New York: the good and the bad, the facts and the fantasy, and the process that turned those facts into that fantasy. The shanghai made Albert Hicks almost admirable, a suitable hero for the immigrant slums.

I have pursued this story for twenty years, chased it in the way of a hobbyist or a private detective. In piecing it together, I made use of city records, articles, and books, but I relied primarily on the transcripts of the court case, as well as Hicks's confession, which was published, along with articles about the arrest and the hanging, in a slim volume called *The Life, Trial, Confession and Execution of Albert W. Hicks.* I backed up, filled out, and corroborated those details with articles and documents published at the time and in the years that followed—some from still-familiar papers like the *New York Post* and the *New York Times,* some from long-defunct papers whose names are as resonant as names on the sides of old clipper ships: the *Brooklyn Eagle,* the *New York Ledger,* the *Police Gazette.* For the greater context of the story, which is America on the eve of the Civil War, I relied on census and crime figures available in archives and records, the Library of Congress, and dozens of books—some new, some old—which can be found, along with the most help-ful newspaper articles, in the bibliography.

I have lived near and visited the streets where these events took place, though many have been rerouted and renamed, paved into something entirely different. Even the Hudson River is not the same—it's smaller and tamer, transformed for the needs of the modern citizen. Every now and then, though, you stumble across a Manhattan building that has somehow survived every upheaval, change, and disaster—the draft riots and garbage strikes, the terror attacks and blackouts—yet still stands, conjuring up that ancient pirate city. For a moment, standing before the Fraunces Tavern at 54 Pearl Street, say, or the Edward Mooney House at 18 Bowery, you get a sense of New York as it was in the time of Albert Hicks. It was not really that long ago. My father was born in 1933. In his childhood, an old man—someone he could have spoken to in a candy store in Bensonhurst, Brooklyn, near where the *E. A. Johnson* laid up, waiting for the wind—might have been a boy in the crowd that watched the last pirate swing.

BIBLIOGRAPHY

BOOKS

Annbinder, Tyler. *City of Dreams: The 400 Year Epic History of Immigrant New York*. New York: Houghton Mifflin Harcourt, 2016.

———. *Five Points: The 19th-Century New York City Neighborhood That Invented Tap Dance, Stole Elections, and Became the World's Most Notorious Slum*. New York: Free Press, 2001.

Asbury, Herbert. *All Around Town: Murder, Scandal, Riot and Mayhem in Old New York*. New York: Knopf, 1929.

———. *Gangs of New York: An Informal History of the Underworld*. New York: Alfred A. Knopf, 1927.

———. *Suckers Progress: An Informal History of Gambling in America*. New York: Dodd Mead, 1938.

Astor, Gerald. *The New York Cops: An Informal History*. New York: Charles Scribner's Sons, 1971.

Banner, Stuart. *The Death Penalty: An American History*. Cambridge, MA: Harvard University Press, 2002.

Barnum, P. T. *Barnum's Own Story.* New York: Dover, 2017.

Beckert, Sven. *The Modern Metropolis: New York City and the Consolidation of the American Bourgeoisie 1850–1896.* Cambridge, UK: Cambridge University Press, 2001.

Booth, Martin. *Opium: A History.* New York: St. Martin's Griffin, 1996.

Brands, H. W. *The Age of Gold: The California Gold Rush and the American Dream.* New York: Anchor, 2003.

Browne, Henri Junius. *The Great Metropolis: A Mirror of New York.* Toledo, OH: R. W. Bliss, 1869.

Bruno, Joe. *Mobsters, Gangs, Crooks, and Other Creeps.* Vol. 1: *New York City.* New York: Knickerbocker Literary Services, 2013.

Burrows, Edwin G., and Mike Wallace: *Gotham: A History of New York City to 1898.* New York: Oxford University Press, 2000.

Cannato, Vincent J. *American Passage: The History of Ellis Island.* New York: Harper Perennial, 2010.

Chadwick, Bruce. *Law & Disorder: The Chaotic Birth of the NYPD.* New York: St. Martin's Press, 2017.

The College of St. Francis Xavier: A Memorial and a Retrospect, 1847–1897. New York: Palala, 2018.

Connors, Chuck. *Bowery Life.* New York City: Franklin Square, 1904.

Crain, Esther. *The Gilded Age in New York, 1870–1910.* Black Dog & Leventhal, 2016.

De Angelis, Lorenzo. *The Life, Trial, Confession and Execution of Albert W. Hicks, The Pirate and Murderer.* New York City: De Witt, 1860.

De Stefano, Anthony M. *Gangland New York: The Places and Faces of Mob History.* London: Rowman & Littlefield, 2015.

Dickens, Charles. *American Notes.* New York: Penguin Classics, 2000.

Dolin, Eric J. *Leviathan: The History of Whaling in America.* New York: W. W. Norton, 2007.

Fleming, Candace. *The Great and Only Barnum: The Tremendous, Stupendous Life of the Showman P. T. Barnum.* New York: Schwartz & Wade, 2009.

Fowler, O. S., and L. N. Fowler. *Phrenology: A Practical Guide to Your Head*. New York: Chelsea House, 1969.

Howe, William F. *Danger! A True History of a Great City's Wiles and Temptations—The Veil Lifted, and Light Thrown on Crime and Its Causes*. Buffalo, NY: Courier, 1886.

Irving, Washington. *A History of New York*. 1809; New York: Penguin Classics, 2008.

Jackson, Kenneth T., ed. *The Encyclopedia of New York*, 2nd ed. New Haven, CT: Yale University Press, 2010.

Katz, Helena. *Gang Wars: Blood and Guts on the Streets of New York*. Canmore, Alberta: Altitude, 2005.

Koeppel, Gerard. *City on a Grid: How New York Became New York*. New York: Da Capo Press, 2015.

Koolhaas, Rem. *Delirious New York*. Italy: Monacelli, 1994.

Kunhardt, Philip, Jr., Phillip B. Kunhardt III, and Peter W. Kunhardt. *P. T. Barnum: America's Greatest Showman*. New York: Knopf, 1995.

Mawer, Granville Allen. *Ahab's Trade: The Saga of South Seas Whaling*. New York: Palgrave Macmillan, 2000.

Morris, Lloyd. *Incredible New York: High Life and Low Life from 1850 to 1950*. Syracuse, NY: Syracuse University Press, 1951.

Richardson, James F. *The New York Police: Colonial Times to 1901*. New York: Oxford University Press, 1970.

Ridge, John Rollin. *Life and Adventures of Joaquín Murieta: Celebrated California Bandit*. Norman: University of Oklahoma Press, 1977.

Riis, Jacob. *How the Other Half Lives*. New York: Charles Scribner's Sons, 1890.

Ruff, Joshua, and Michael Cronin. *New York City Police: Images of America*. New York: Arcadia, 2012.

Sante, Luc. *Low Life: Lures and Snares of Old New York*. New York: Farrar, Straus & Giroux, 1991.

Schechter, Harold. *Psycho USA: Famous American Killers You Never Heard Of*. New York: Ballantine Books, 2012.

Shorto, Russell. *The Island at the Center of the World*. New York: Doubleday, 2004.

Steinberg, Ted. *Gotham Unbound: The Ecological History of Greater New York*. New York: Simon & Schuster, 2014.

Stevenson, Robert Louis. *In the South Seas*. 1896; rpt. Floating Press, 2009.

———. *Kidnapped*. 1886; rpt. London: Oxford University Press, 2014.

———. *Travels in Hawaii*. Honolulu: University of Hawaii Press, 1973.

———. *Treasure Island*. 1883; rpt. New York: Penguin Classics, 1999.

Strausbaugh, John. *City of Sedition: The History of New York City During the Civil War*. New York: Twelve, 2016.

Sutton, Charles. *The New York Tombs: Its Secrets and Its Mysteries*. New York: United States Publishing Co., 1874.

Thebaud, Augustus J. *Forty Years in the United States of America, 1839–1885*. New York: United States Catholic Historical Society, 1902.

Tosches, Nick. *The Last Opium Den*. New York: Bloomsbury, 2000.

Van Every, Edward. *Sins of New York: As Exposed by the Police Gazette*. New York: Frederic A. Stokes Co., 1930.

Whalen, Bernard, Philip Messing, and Robert Mladinich. *Undisclosed Files of the Police: Cases from the Archives of the NYPD from 1831 to the Present*. New York: Black Dog & Leventhal, 2016.

Whalen, Bernard, and Jon Whalen. *The NYPD's First Fifty Years: Politicians, Police Commissioners, and Patrolmen*. Lincoln: University of Nebraska Press, 2014.

Willoughby, Edward. *Early Street Gangs and Gangsters of New York, 1800–1919*. Middletown, DE, 2016.

Young, Green, and Tom Meyers. *The Bowery Boys: Adventures in Old New York*. Berkeley, CA: Ulysses Press, 2016.

ARTICLES AND DOCUMENTS

"Captain Rynders and the Lone Star." *New York Times,* March 15, 1855.

"Tammany Troubles.; Another Grand Battle—Royal in Tammany

Hall. The Vermilion, Edict Repudiated, The Last Vestige of Mayor Wood Wiped Out. Meddling Country Politicians Instructed. The Indepndence and Dignity of the Demeoratic Party Vindicated." *New York Times,* July 27, 1857.

"Serenade to Marshal Rynders; The Marshal's Opinion of Serenades, and of the Sycophants who Generally Get Them Up." *New York Times,* June 24, 1858.

"Law Reports. Murder Trials. Verdict of Guilty Against John Crummins for the Murder of Dennis McHenry—Trial of Mortimer Shay for the Murder of John Leary." *New York Times,* February 2, 1860.

"Great Eastern—The Steamship Great Eastern Is on Exhibition." *New York Post,* March 14, 1860.

"News of the Day." *New York Times,* March 15, 1860.

"Arrest of Twenty-Four Females in Broadway." *New York Post,* March 16, 1860.

"The Jury and the Press." *New York Times,* March 16, 1860.

"Alexander Dumas in Italy." *New York Post,* March 20, 1860.

"Law Reports. The Sloop Murders. Conviction of Albert W. Hicks, alias Wm. Johnson, for Robbery on the High Seas." *New York Times,* March 21, 1860.

"The Case of the Abandoned Schooner." *New York Post,* March 22, 1860.

Extradition Notice: "I, Albert W. Hicks, agree to go New-York with Officer George Nevins, of my own free will and accord. (Signed) Albert W. Hicks." City Marshal's Office, Providence, RI, March 24, 1860.

"The Murders on the Oyster Sloop." *New York Times,* March 24, 1860.

"Alleged Horrible Cruelty on Shipboard." *New York Post,* March 26, 1860.

"The Lower Bay Tragedy—Positive Identification of the Prisoner—He Is Taken to the U.S. Marshal's Office and Examined on the Charge of Piracy—The Latest and Fullest Particulars." *Brooklyn Daily Eagle,* March 26, 1860.

"News of the Day." *New York Times,* March 26, 1860.

"News of the Day." *New York Times,* March 27, 1860.

"The Tragedies at Sea. The Two Alleged Murderers in Custody." *New York Times,* March 27, 1860.

"The Oyster-Sloop Tragedy." *New York Post,* March 28, 1860.

"News Story." *Evening Post,* March 28, 1860.

"The Murders at Sea. Examination of Hicks—Additional Evidence Against Him." *New York Times,* March 29, 1860.

"News of the Day." *New York Times,* March 31, 1860.

"New York City News." *Brooklyn Eagle,* March 31, 1860.

"City Intelligence. The Cheever Quarrel. Continuation of the Debate Remarks by Messrs. Blankman, Berry and Gilbert." *New York Times,* May 15, 1860.

"Law Reports. The Sloop Murders. Trial of Albert W. Hicks, alias Wm. Johnson, Indicted for Robbery on the High Seas." *New York Times,* May 16, 1860.

"Law Reports. The Sloop Murders. Trial of Albert W. Hicks, alias Wm. Johnson, Indicted for Robbery on the High Seas." *New York Times,* May 17, 1860.

"Law Reports. The Sloop Murders. Trial of Albert W. Hicks, Alias Wm. Johnson, for Robbery on the High Seas." *New York Times,* May 19, 1860.

"Trial Notes." *New York Evening Express,* 1860.

"Letter to the Editor." *New York Times,* June 3, 1860.

"The Sloop Murders.; Albert W. Hicks Sentenced to Death. Letters from His Brother and the Mother of His Wife—Verses by the Prisoner, Indicating a Previous Crime." *New York Times,* June 2, 1860.

"News of the Day." *New York Times,* June 2, 1860.

"The Oyster Sloop Murders. Further Developments in the Life of Hicks. The Tragedy of the Saladin Interesting Details of a Past Tragedy." *New York Times,* June 4, 1860.

"The Oyster Sloop Murders." *Evening Post,* June 6, 1860.

"New York City News." *Brooklyn Eagle,* June 6, 1860.

"The Murders on the Oyster Sloop. A Partial Confession from Hicks—He Admits His Guilt and Details Some of the Particulars of the Tragedy." *New York Times,* June 6, 1860.

"Changes in the United States District Attorney's Office." *New York Times,* June 19, 1860.

"Political Affairs." *New York Herald,* July 9, 1860.

"The Execution To-Day." *New York Post,* July 13, 1860.

"Pirate Hicks Is Executed," *New York Daily Tribune,* July 14, 1860.

"Execution of Hicks, the Pirate. Twelve Thousand People at Bedloe's Island. Scenes at the Tombs, in the Bay, and at the Place of Execution. His Confession." *New York Times,* July 14, 1860.

"Charge of Judge Smalley on the Slave-trade; United States Circuit Court Dec. 26." *New York Times,* December 27, 1860.

"Rynders and Roosevelt." *New York Times,* March 26, 1861.

"From Gen. Stone's Division.; Shelling at Monocacy—Rebel Cavalry Dispersed—The Baker Brigade—Official List of Killed and Wounded in California Regiment—Soldier's Funeral—Honorable Mention—Col. Geary's Regiment on the Move—Correction of Heraldic Statements. The Baker Brigade, A Muffled Drum Capt. Elias Smith." *New York Times,* October 29, 1861.

Genin, John N. "The Origins and History of the Kossuth Hat." *Harper's Weekly,* March 1862.

"NYPD: Forgotten History. The Establishment of the Harbor Police or 24th Precinct by the Metropolitan Police Department." Policeny.com.

"Praise of Cap't Rynders; Traits in his Character That a Minister Found to Admire." *New York Times,* January 13, 1885.

"Isaiah Rynders." Obituary. *Chicago Tribune,* January 14, 1885.

"Father Henry Duranquet." Obituary. *Messenger of the Sacred Heart,* April 1886.

"Father Dominic Du Ranquet: A Sketch of his Life and Labors, 1813–1900." *Jesuit Online Library.*

"In the Catholic Churches." *New York Times,* August 22, 1887.

Van Wye, John. *The History of Phrenology.* http://www.history ofphrenology.org.uk/fowlers.htm.

Berger, Meyer. "The Tombs—II." *The New Yorker,* September 6, 1941.

ABOUT THE AUTHOR

RICH COHEN is the author of the *New York Times* bestsellers *Tough Jews; Monsters; Sweet and Low; When I Stop Talking, You'll Know I'm Dead* (with Jerry Weintraub); *The Sun & the Moon & the Rolling Stones;* and *The Chicago Cubs: Story of a Curse*. He is a cocreator of the HBO series *Vinyl* and a contributing editor at *Vanity Fair* and *Rolling Stone* and has written for *The New Yorker, The Atlantic,* and *Harper's Magazine,* among other publications. Cohen has won the Great Lakes Book Award, the Chicago Public Library Foundation's 21st Century Award, and the ASCAP Deems Taylor Award for outstanding coverage of music. His stories have been included in *The Best American Essays* and *The Best American Travel Writing*. Despite frequent predictions, he still lives in Connecticut.

authorrichcohen.com
Facebook.com/rich.cohen1
Twitter: @richcohen2003

ABOUT THE TYPE

This book was set in Sabon, a typeface designed by the well-known German typographer Jan Tschichold (1902–74). Sabon's design is based upon the original letter forms of sixteenth-century French type designer Claude Garamond and was created specifically to be used for three sources: foundry type for hand composition, Linotype, and Monotype. Tschichold named his typeface for the famous Frankfurt typefounder Jacques Sabon (c. 1520–80).